Flutter, Skitter, and Skim

Flutter, Skitter, and Skim

Using the Living Insect as a Guide to Successful Fly Fishing

Leonard M. Wright Jr.

THE DERRYDALE PRESS

LANHAM AND NEW YORK

THE DERRYDALE PRESS

Published in the United States of America
by The Derrydale Press
4720 Boston Way, Lanham, Maryland 20706

Distributed by NATIONAL BOOK NETWORK, INC.

Library of Congress Cataloging-in-Publication Data

Wright, Leonard M.
    Flutter, skitter, and skim : Using the living insect as a guide for successful
fly fishing / Leonard M. Wright, Jr. ; illustrated by Norman Adams.
        p.   cm.
    Originally published: 1st ed, New York : Dutton, 1972.
    ISBN 1-58667-053-0 (pbk. : alk. paper)
    1. Fly fishing. 2. Trout fishing. 3. Flies, Artificial. I. Title.
SH456.W7 2000
799.1'24—dc21   00-059032

CONTENTS

FISHING THE DRY FLY
AS A LIVING INSECT

PREFACE

Some younger readers may find this hard to believe, but in 1972 when this book was first published, you couldn't find a floating caddis pattern in any fly shop. And the idea of fishing the dry fly in any way other than Halford's dead drift was so heretical that I wanted to title the book *A Fly-Fishing Heresy*. (The editor overruled me in favor of the title *Fishing the Dry Fly as a Living Insect*.)

This slim volume really woke up the fly fishing fraternity. The great Red Smith devoted two of his widely syndicated columns to it one week. It was given a major review on the sports pages of the weekday *New York Times* and received several paragraphs of comment in their Sunday Book Review. For two or three years, Orvis gave a full page in their catalogue to offering both the book and patterns of my all-hackle "Fluttering Caddis" imitations. The book went through four printings and sold some 25,000 copies, which was a lot for a fishing book in those days.

I bring this up because the book is mostly forgotten, now, twenty-eight years later. The reason for this is simple: tying on a downwing floater and fishing it with a slight twitch are such accepted practices today that their origins—though actually relatively recent—seem to belong to a misty, distant past.

So I'll have to admit to those who buy and read this book that they're not likely to pick up vast amounts of new information. But then they probably won't if they read Halford's *Dry Fly Fishing in Theory and Practice* or Skues' *Chalk Stream Angler*, either.

And yet, a fly-fishing library would seem incomplete without both of them, wouldn't it?

1

THE FLY
THAT FISHERMEN FORGOT

Memory is especially merciful to fishermen. We relive our successful days astream over and over again, while our fishless hours are easily forgotten. And yet I think we pay a high price for this kindness since it is our failures that teach us. I have never learned anything on days when fishing was easy, while the most galling defeat I've ever suffered on a river started me thinking, reading, observing, experimenting. I'm sure, now, that my trout fishing education really began on a disastrous day in early June and this is the way it happened.

It was a surprisingly raw, gusty afternoon for that time of year and I had been fishing the lower Beaver Kill since midmorning without raising a fish. Only the fact that I had driven 125 miles to get there and that a return trip faced me at the end of the day kept me doggedly at it so long.

Shortly after six o'clock, when I was finally ready to give up, a dramatic change occurred: the wind dropped abruptly and there was a sudden softness to the air. For one of the few times in my life I sensed, with that instinctive awareness most animals seem to have, that something important in nature was about to happen. I can remember standing there uneasily, wondering if a tornado were about to come over one of the surrounding hills.

Within minutes the air was full of hawking swallows and then I saw them. Flies—first by twos and threes, next by dozens and finally by the hundreds and thousands —started swarming past me upstream, the highest thirty feet or more above my head and the lowest richocheting along the water surface. Never before or since have I seen such a hatch! The flat water around me began to churn with feeding trout, some leaping, some slashing, some just lipping the surface.

I tied on a #14 Quill Gordon—a fly that seemed about right in size and color—and went to work on a large trout I'd marked down. Up he came again and again, yet I have never had my fly so pointedly ignored. He picked off naturals so close to my Quill that he rocked it several times. Once he even bunted it with his nose. But he never made the fatal mistake.

I switched to other, smaller trout nearby, but the result was the same. As darkness fell, I was casting with random desperation hoping for one foolish fish of any size. I must have covered more than a hundred rising trout during that two-hour feeding orgy without a single take! I have been blanked before and since, but never in the midst of such plenty. I finally left the river in pitch darkness, arm-weary, chagrinned, bewildered.

During this shambles I had done one thing that was right, though. I had stopped casting long enough to trap a few specimens with my hat and stuff them into a fly box. Later that night I examined my captives as they crawled through a compartment filled with Quill Gordons. The color hadn't been a bad match, after all, and the size #14 seemed about right, too. But the shape, especially the silhouette, was as wrong as it possibly could be. The naturals had wings that seemed solid or opaque and were furled horizontally, enveloping the body. And these insects had no tails, but long feelers in front. All the flies in my boxes, on the other hand, had long tails and translucent wings that were set bolt-upright, perpendicular to the body. Like most dry flies dressed today, all my artificials had been tied to imitate some mayfly or other, and mayflies look nothing at all like the flies I'd just captured. The latter belonged to a different order of insects called the Trichoptera, or caddis flies.

In fact, not one of the fifty or one hundred most popular dry flies of today is tied in the distinctive caddis shape. You can look through store after store and not find a single floating imitation of an adult caddis. Yet, the caddis runs the mayfly a close second as the trout's most important insect food. Dr. Paul Needham, in his 1938 study of *Trout Streams*, noted that while the brown trout autopsied had more mayfly nymphs and adults in their stomachs than caddis, brook trout, in the same streams, had eaten more

Dark Blue Caddis   #14 Quill Gordon

caddis than mayflies. No other insect type was even close to the caddis for the combined second place. But Needham's excellent studies were made on small streams and these never seem to have the profuse caddis hatches that rivers do.

I wonder how the proportions would have worked out if, for example, he had sampled the trout on a river like the lower Beaver Kill over an entire season. On this river the shad fly, *Brachycentrus*, alone hatches out in far greater numbers than both the famous Quill Gordon and Hendrickson mayflies put together. The blue caddis, *Psilotreta*, in June overshadows any mayfly hatch on that river during that month. As a result, I am convinced that on many large, slightly acid waters, caddis flies will give the much publicized mayflies a very close race for first place as the top trout food.

Ernest Schwiebert has published some figures on trout autopsies conducted more recently which show that not only has the caddis-mayfly ratio swung over toward the caddis side since Needham's time, but that this is a continuing trend. Schwiebert feels this is happening because increasing pollution and the wider use of pesticides are taking a higher toll of the relatively fragile mayflies while sparing the more rugged caddis. Whatever the reason, it appears that caddis are not only extremely important as trout food today, but that they may well become even more so in the years ahead!

And yet, caddis are seldom mentioned in books on trout flies. This baffles me. The three best-known fishermen's entomologies published in this country seem to agree that caddis flies aren't important to fishermen. Ernest Schwiebert's excellent *Matching the Hatch* devotes three pages and two black-and-white drawings to caddis. Art Flick doesn't even mention them in his *Streamside Guide*. Preston Jennings does somewhat better in *A Book of Trout Flies*. He gives eight pages of text and several drawings to three types of caddis flies, but he is noticeably unenthusiastic about an angler's chances of success when fishing these hatches. A friend of mine who used to fish with Jennings tells me he once asked the author why he gave this section such skimpy treatment. Preston's reply was, "Well, nobody really *cares* about caddis." Actually, all three of these authors were very familiar with Catskill fishing in general and with the Beaver Kill in particular and had to be well aware of the great caddis hatches that occur throughout the region.

Louis Rhead, writing near the turn of the century, did face up to the caddis problem, even though he couldn't come up with a solution. He devoted a large section of his book, *American Trout-Stream Insects*, to one species of caddis alone. "The Shad-fly is the most abundant trout insect-food that appears on our Eastern and some Middle and Far Western streams. Trout are ravenous for it. When the Shad-fly is on the water you will never fail to see trout rising," he wrote. But he added, "When the great rise appears it is hardly possible to catch a trout with any prevailing artificial as now tied."

Obviously, American trout fishing was suffering from an acute case of caddis-neglect and the more I thought about it the more I became intrigued with this insect. I began leafing through fishing books to track down exactly when and why the plentiful caddis fly had been written off. This turned out to be more difficult than I had expected because terminology was rather vague 100 years ago and early American fishing writers—up through Gordon and even LaBranche—seldom mentioned whether the fly they were describing was a caddis fly, mayfly or stone fly. However, it soon became apparent that the caddis had played a pivotal role in American fly fishing right up until Rhead's time. The wet flies used by nineteenth-century fishermen were good imitations of the shape of adult caddis and some of the specific patterns like the White Miller, Montreal and Grizzly King were tied to the colors of individual species. But the way in which these flies were manipulated gives the strongest proof that the caddis played a major part in last century's fishing repertory.

Perhaps a brief review of our ancestors' fishing techniques, at this point, can provide some clues to the case of the disappearing caddis.

By the time trout fishing emerged as a sport in America, the mills and fish-gathering of colonial times had already taken their toll. Contrary to popular belief, mid-nineteenth-century sportsmen did not live in a fisherman's paradise. Already, most major rivers in the Northeast had been dammed or polluted beyond the tolerance of salmon or trout. Small streams near home may have still run clear, cool and uncluttered by tin cans, but they had been overfished and now held only tiddling brook trout best left to small boys and village idlers.

Yet, there remained a vast semiwilderness not too far away. Real fishing meant a trip to Maine, to the Adirondacks or on to Canada. Here were chains of clear lakes or peaty ponds relatively unfished by today's standards and teeming with wild brook trout. Weekend buggy excursions were out of the question; this sort of fishing meant long trips with guides and long stays under canvas. Winslow Homer caught the end of this era and his watercolors can tell us as much about it as any book.

Sportsmen fished these waters the same way their ances-

tors had fished the lakes and lochs of Great Britain—
with a technique that is used on the other side of the Atlantic to this day. Three wet flies were cast from a drifting
boat and then retrieved with the rod tip held high so that
the top dropper bounced across the surface like an adult
caddis. At midday, waves gave plenty of life to the fly,
but, in the dead calm of dusk, the rod tip was often wig-
gled to give the dropper more action. This transplanted
technique worked, and worked well, here because caddis
are major food insects in acid waters on both sides of the
ocean.

This kind of fishing was on the way out even eighty
years ago and you'd have to look far and wide to witness it
anywhere in America today. Three events occurred in
rapid succession that were to change American fly fishing,
perhaps, forever.

First came the transplanting of the smallmouth black
bass from the Mississippi watershed into the lakes of the
Northeast. Bass are great gamefish in their own right, but
they're too much competition for the slower-growing
brook trout. Squaretail populations dropped off rapidly in
the newly stocked waters and the lakes that still held trout
just couldn't absorb the increased pressure. Despite vigorous restocking policies, still-water trout fishing in New
York and New England hasn't recovered to this day.

Second, the hardy, fast-growing brown trout from Europe was introduced into our larger, less-polluted streams
at about the same time. Why travel all the way to the
now-uncertain waters of Northern Maine when you could
catch three-pound trout after a two or three hour train
ride? Advanced fly-fishers turned to the challenge of
brown trout and began to focus on running-water techniques.

Third, well-informed anglers quickly borrowed more sophisticated European methods to deal with these imported trout. In came the new orthodoxy fresh from the pages of Halford and the chalk streams of England. The long, limber rods and light lines used for lake fishing began to gather dust in attics. The new rod must be stiff, the line heavy, the leader tapered to the finest point. The single fly must float and float absolutely dead drift.

Halford's dry-fly theory captured the imaginations of our fly-fishers and, needless to say, it worked on the brown trout in our waters, too. Yet something had been lost. True, men like Gordon, LaBranche and Hewitt modified chalk-stream dogma to suit American conditions and they made magnificent contributions. But perhaps they didn't go far enough because they all forgot the caddis.

Probably the most logical explanation for this enormous omission is that these great fishermen all started with Halford's doctrine and changed it only when necessity dictated. *It is interesting to speculate on what American dry-fly fishing would have been like today if it had sprung up spontaneously under our conditions and on our rivers.* Consider the gap that must be bridged between the Test in Hampshire, England, and, say, the Beaver Kill in New York. The Test is one of the richest rivers in the world, chemically. It never suffers from scouring floods and is literally paved with weeds and teems with insect life. The Beaver Kill, on the other hand, is acid, lacking the rich carbonates of chalk streams. It is subjected to several destructive floods every year and produces almost no waterweed. Obviously, the ecology and entomology of this spartan environment differs widely from those of the Test. Mayfly life is much less profuse, while the acid-tolerant caddis takes on added importance.

Admittedly, the Test has a good caddis population, too. But with endless squadrons of mayfly duns floating down to waiting trout, Halford gave caddis a very minor place. They were rowdy intruders into his serenely ordered scheme of things. He grudgingly included five caddis patterns in his final selection of forty-three dry flies as some sort of last-ditch remedy when darkness and total defeat were closing in on the angler. Mayfly imitations and the fishing of them absolutely drag-free occupied Halford's missionary zeal for the last twenty years of his influential life.

But at least Halford carried five caddis dry-fly patterns. Can the American trouter, who casts his flies on waters where caddis abound, afford to ignore this type of fly completely? And why, with so many caddis buzzing around him and with their prevalence increasing yearly, does he continue to do so?

I think most anglers simply fail to recognize caddis when they see them. They may be familiar with the log-cabin cases of the larvae and quite able to pick out the winged adult in an illustration. But many otherwise expert anglers are weak on "aircraft identification" and it is surprising how few bother to capture specimens for a closer look. Yet the three basic types of aquatic insects that interest fishermen most are easy to identify on the wing, even at a considerable distance.

Stone flies are awkward flyers and hold their bodies in a nearly vertical position while their four wings, all of which are visible separately, seem to flail the air. The identity of a captured specimen can be confirmed by the two short tails and by the fact that the wings fold flat, at rest, parallel to, and on top of, the body.

Mayfly duns are weak but steady flyers, appear to have

two translucent wings and hold their bodies horizontally when in flight. After a day or so they undergo a transformation, shedding a fine outer skin, and becoming imagoes or spinners. They are now even more translucent and have become agile flyers as they dance over the water for mating, but are still clearly distinguishable as mayflies. In both stages they have two or three long, hairlike tails and carry their wings erect, like Marconi-rigged sails, over their backs when at rest.

Adult caddis flies look very much like moths in the air and are strong though erratic flyers. Their wings appear opaque and their prominent antennae are visible from quite some distance. When not flying, their wings are folded over, but parallel to, their bodies in an inverted V. All caddis are clearly distinguishable from the previous two aquatic insects because they have no setae or tails.

Even from these capsulized descriptions, the average angler should be able to identify at a glance ninety percent of the insects he sees on the stream. Yet it's amazing how few fishermen try to make even this simple diagnosis. Most swarms of caddis flies are shrugged off as "brush hatches"

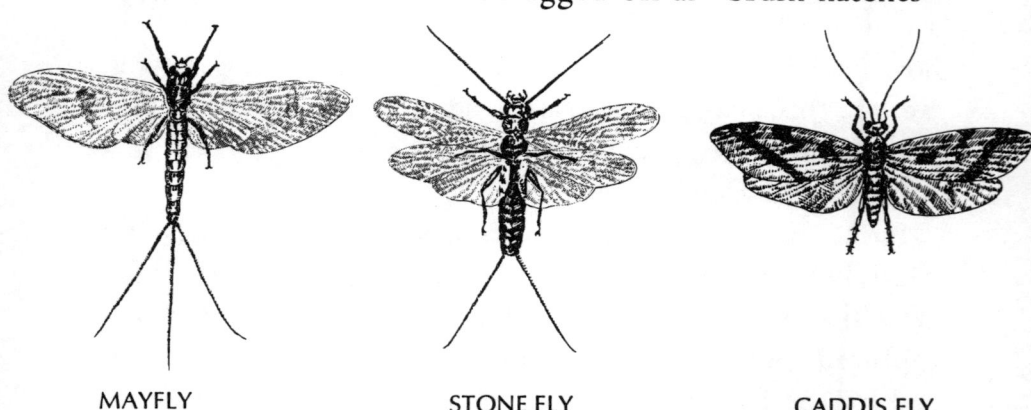

MAYFLY   STONE FLY   CADDIS FLY

Aquatic Insects in Flight

—meaning that all the flies are coming out of the bushes instead of off the water and therefore the trout aren't the least bit interested in them. Many of the insects may, indeed, be coming from the bushes, as most caddis live for several weeks as adults and return to the river each evening for mating or egg-laying. But that's no reason for crossing them off. Very likely some more of the same species are hatching out that evening and many of the previously hatched flies will be buzzing the surface enticingly.

The other main reason why caddis flies are too often ignored by anglers is that their coverage in fishing books has been sparing, to put it mildly. Occasionally there is some general mention of wet-fly fishing in fast or streamy water to take fish feeding on emerging pupae. Yet the Ed Sens pupal imitations represent one of the few American attempts to deal seriously with caddis flies in any form. Dry-fly imitation of the adult caddis is usually dismissed or omitted, first, because caddis are seen more often in the air than on the water and are, therefore, seldom available to trout and, second, because most caddis are said to hatch after dark when the fisherman has gone home.

Unfortunately, there's just enough truth in both of these observations to have discouraged serious experimentation. But do they stand up under close scrutiny? Aren't mayflies also noticed more often when flying than when floating quietly downstream? Isn't it perhaps true that we see more mayflies on the water because their upright wings make them far more visible than the low-profile caddis? And don't most mayflies also hatch in late evening—or at night—once the blustery days of early spring are over? I think the answer to these questions has to be "Yes."

So much for the defensive. There are several more positive arguments in favor of imitating the adult caddis flies.

They are not only more plentiful, as we have seen, but caddis lead much longer adult lives than mayflies—weeks instead of days. As a result, trout get many more chances to see or rise to each individual insect. And caddis flies are, apparently, especially delicious. I have noticed that some species of mayflies are rarely taken by trout—some stone flies are actually avoided by them—but I have never seen a caddis that wasn't eaten with relish, often in preference to a well-known mayfly that was hatching out simultaneously.

And that pretty much winds up the case for the caddis flies. They are very important to trout. Yet most trout-fishers continue to ignore them simply because their training has led them to do so.

Arizona Game and Fish Department
2221 W. Greenway Rd.
Phoenix, AZ 85023
(602) 942-3000

Region I
2878 E. White Mountain
Pinetop, AZ 85935
(520) 367-4281

Region II
3500 S. Lake Mary Rd.
Flagstaff, AZ 86001
(520) 774-5045

Region III
5325 N. Stockton Hill Rd.
Kingman, AZ 86401
(520) 692-7700

Region IV
9140 E. County 10 1/2 St.
Yuma, AZ 85365
(520) 342-0091

Region V
555 N. Greasewood Rd.
Tucson, AZ 85745
(520) 628-5376

Region VI
7200 E. University Ave.
Mesa, AZ 85207
(480) 981-9400

Hunters, shooters and anglers support Sport Fish and Wildlife Restoration Programs through an excise tax on the purchase of firearms, ammunition and fishing equipment. Thank you hunters, shooters and anglers for funding wildlife conservation and habitat protection projects in Arizona!

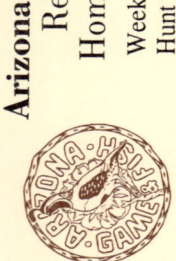

Arizona Game and Fish Department

Resource Information Card

Home Page - www.gf.state.az.us

Weekly Wildlife News - (602) 789-3700
Hunt Information Line - (602) 789-3702

Weekly Arizona Fishing Report - (602) 789-3701

Fishing Information for Arizona and Other States - 1-800-ASK-FISH

Ben Avery Shooting Facility - (602) 582-8313

Adobe Mountain Wildlife Center - (602) 789-3371

To Report Wildlife Violations - Operation Game Thief - 1-800-352-0700

To Report Vandalism or Livestock Depredation - 1-800-VANDALS

FAX-ON-Request Line - Dial (602) 530-2210 with appropriate extension:

Directory Of All Documents	777	Hunter Education Courses	4007
Weekly Wildlife News	4000	Fishing Clinics	4008
Weekly Fishing Report	4001	Watchable Wildlife Trips	4009
Fish Stocking Schedule	3010	Hunt Drawing Application	2000
Lake Elevations	3009	Leftover Permits Remaining	2008
			2008

2

HINTS OF HERESY

My own early trout fishing education, if you can dignify such a hit or miss process with that word, was essentially Halfordian. I hadn't read Halford as a child, of course, and I probably hadn't even heard of him, but I seem to have absorbed his doctrine by osmosis in small doses from chance conversations and from fishing catalogues or magazines. The theory I then subscribed to, as I now remember it, went something like this. There will be a large hatch of mayflies at a certain time of day. When this occurs, you must tie on a dry fly that looks exactly like the fly on the water and cast it in an upstream direction so that it floats back freely and naturally over the nose of a feeding trout which will then rise and sip it in.

That was real trout fishing. Catching trout on wet flies or bucktails—even taking a trout by chance on a dry fly—was little better than worm fishing. I remember waiting for this promised glut of mayfly every time I fished. I felt that I must be doing something wrong—

that I was at the wrong place at the wrong time or that I was woefully unobservant—because I met these ideal conditions only once in a blue moon. Most of the time I fished catch-as-catch-can, overshadowed by the dark feeling that my beautiful young soul had, through some unknown though probably original sin, been reincarnated in the body of a congenital bait-fisher.

Of course, I was fishing Northeastern streams, mostly rundown ones at that, and these are a far cry from the stately chalk streams of England. The best rises of trout I encountered were usually caused by a fall of flying ants or a leap of grasshoppers and this wasn't the real thing at all. I remember catching the odd mayfly in my hat and standing there, holding my breath, waiting for that ultimate dun hatch that would start the water boiling. Almost every trout I caught in those days was like a grouse shot on the ground—meat in the pot, perhaps, but taken by dark and devious means.

During these lean years while I was waiting for trout fishing to become what it was supposed to be, many seemingly unorthodox things happened that started me wondering whether Halfordism wasn't, after all, just a fairy tale from a far-off land. I didn't voice these doubts to other fishermen, though; I was just as ready to admire the Emperor's new clothes as the next man.

The earliest of these experiences occurred when I was a thirteen-year-old at boarding school in upstate New York. There was a deep pool on the Little Hoosac River that I fished again and again because I felt sure it held monster trout. Looking back on it now, I am convinced that I was right although the fish I actually caught there were few, small and far between. The head of this pool was deep and filled with bubbles where the water rushed in and this, I felt, was where the Leviathans had to be hiding.

I had never raised a fish in this hypnotic part of the pool, but I concentrated my efforts here waiting for the lucky strike that would make me a celebrity among my peers. Following one spell of high water, several branches were left jammed between some rocks at the shoulder of the pool on the far bank. A careless cast, one day, wrapped my leader securely around a stout twig, leaving my fly bouncing on the surface of the current some two feet below. This was a serious situation. An expensive tapered gut leader was in jeopardy and so was a store-bought #12 Ginger Quill. Crossing this stream in spring was a major undertaking and as I plotted the shallowest and safest course to the far side, my long-awaited dream came true —or, I should say, almost came true. There was a large splash, a glimpse of the rusty side of a big brown and my retrieval problem was solved—although it left me half a month's allowance poorer in tackle.

I never told my fishing schoolmates about this incident because monsters-that-got-away stories were a favorite art form with us and it didn't seem right to enter a true experience in our running liar's contest. I thought about it a lot before going to sleep at night, though. And after I got over the feeling that the world was against me—that the one time a truly large trout had taken my dry fly was when my line was hopelessly snagged—I started to realize *why* the fish had struck. It stood to reason that a fly hovering in and out of the surface film directly over a trout's head had to be tantalizing, despite the purist dogma of dead drift. But that's as far as I went: At the time I couldn't see any practical application to the expensive and purely accidental research I'd just conducted.

Several years later I had another vivid experience which was to prove slightly more useful. I used to fish a short stretch of Connecticut's Saugatuck River that ran past the house of a friend. At the very bottom of this beat, a small dam created a plunge-pool five or six feet deep which marked the head of a long, slow still-water. Both sides of this small, choice pool were lined with dense willows. If nothing could be raised by letting a wet fly or bucktail swim down from above, I had to press along the edge of this tangle, sometimes taking in water over my boot-tops and roll casting my fly in an across or upstream presentation. This was a difficult and often painful procedure in the high water of April and early May, but it saved me from a blank evening on many occasions. This almost unfishable spot held by far the best trout of any nearby section of the stream.

Even roll casting was a feat in these tight quarters. The rod couldn't be raised quite up to the vertical position because of overhanging branches so the cast had to be executed with a short, violent motion. Getting out thirty feet of line was a bravura performance here and any sort of wind in your face made a decent presentation virtually impossible. You had to slam your fly out into the deepest part of the pool, let it fish for a few feet and then slam it out again. Not delicate fishing, but surprisingly effective in that deep, streamy water.

Of course my rod took an awful beating in there, banging against branches at almost every cast, and one evening I was sure I had smashed it for good. I had been fishing a small, brown bucktail, roll casting it out as usual, when a trout hit the fly almost at my feet as it raced across the surface toward me before flipping up and over in the delayed action that characterizes this type of cast. The old bamboo shuddered and shook under the impact and I stopped to examine it inch by inch with fear and trembling, without giving a moment's thought to the fish. After I was satisfied that the rod had, miraculously, come through unscathed, I began to strip in the line and found a second pleasant surprise: The trout was still on and he was a fine thirteen-incher!

For once in my life, I put two and two together right on the spot. I reasoned that the bucktail, racing across the surface, had stampeded this highly educated trout into striking while the more leisurely underwater presentation hadn't done the job. And while I couldn't improvise a presentation out of the last split second of a roll cast, perhaps I could get much the same effect with more control and less danger to my rod if I could roll cast to a chosen spot, keep my rod tip high as the fly hit the water, then retrieve instantly, before the bucktail had time to sink. There was no chance for a hand retrieve of the line with this method and each cast netted me only a short eight- or ten-foot presentation. But it was enough to take two more trout from this hole in the next half hour before dark and one of these was nearly two inches longer than the first one. From then on, this became my standard delivery when I fished this pool and the results were far better than before. Why I never attempted this presentation in other places, I can't explain. But as far as I can remember I had never tried it on any other pools or streams.

Then there were several days I remember on larger rivers when the trout acted as if they were trying to make fools out of both Halford and me. Nearly every rise I got occurred just as I was about to pick my fly off the water and recast it. This was not only frustrating, but it chewed up terminal tackle at an alarming rate because any decent fish that struck against the tight line snapped the tippet, leaving me to wonder just how big the fish really had been. This maddening experience was most common when

I was fishing long slow flats, casting slightly upward, but mostly across the current. Though I realized that the strikes were occurring just as the dry fly started to drag at the end of the float, I couldn't think of anything I could do about it.

No, on some days trout fishing wasn't what it was supposed to be at all. And I think the crowning experience of this type occurred during the summer of 1945 when some family friends invited me for a two-week stay on a remote lake in a large Adirondack preserve. They told me the lake was teeming with trout, but admitted they didn't fish very often themselves. I arrived in late July with a short, stiff dry fly rod, double tapered silk line, tapered gut leaders, some beautiful prewar, Hardy dry flies and enough self-confidence for the whole party. The feeling that I'd be taking advantage of these unsophisticated brook trout grew when I saw the tackle my hosts were using. Their rods were nine to ten feet long and as limp as grape vines. Windings were frayed and varnish was chipped or nonexistent. Some were made of solid wood and didn't even have cork grips. And that was just the beginning. Reels were toy-sized and held only a few yards of thin, cracked enamel line. On the end of these rigs were the heaviest level leaders I'd ever seen, each sporting a team of three large, snelled wet flies. Everything looked as though it had been borrowed from the Smithsonian. My host admitted that these outfits had been kicking around for years but added that they still worked surprisingly well.

After supper that first evening, six of us piled into three canoes and paddled uplake to a wide, alder-lined inlet flowage. I immediately began casting a perky little dry fly to likely looking spots, but, to my astonishment, I didn't see or get a rise. The others just chatted together quietly and didn't bother to pick up their rods until just at dusk when caddis flies and rising trout appeared as suddenly as if some hidden signal had been given. I soon noticed, to my chagrin, that everyone else was hauling in fish. My frequently cast dry fly just sat there rocking on the ripples set up by the trout rising all around it. The others were making ridiculously short casts and trickling the flies back over the surface often not more than a dozen feet from their canoes. And they were hooking fish almost every time they cast.

If I remember correctly, everyone else caught a dozen or more fat, dark trout running from half a pound to slightly more than a pound, while I managed to land one six-incher just at dark. Needless to say, I borrowed one of those archaic rigs and learned how to dance the dropper properly, making it zigzag over the surface like the caddis flies that miraculously appeared at the same hour each evening.

Actually, what I had been witnessing was the old, mid-nineteenth-century lake fishing technique that I mentioned briefly in the previous chapter. And, although the tackle used may seem primitive to today's fishermen, it was ideally suited to its task. Perhaps we may be able to learn something about fish-taking techniques from this presentation. The rod was long to keep the flies as far as possible from the boat. It was limber to impart a jiggling motion to the dropper and to prevent a smash when a large fish walloped the fly. The line was light and level to keep it from bellying down close to the boat, and the flies were on heavy snells so that they would stand out away from the leader and dance properly. The heaviness of the leader itself didn't seem to put the fish off because the two bottom flies were rarely taken. Their main function was to set up enough drag in the water to tighten line and leader during the retrieve. When the rod was held high and the tip was wobbled by the angler, the skittering top dropper captured the trout's attention. When you see this stunt performed properly you realize that the hand of man can't better this impression of a caddis buzzing over the surface.

This experience, dramatic as it was, made little impression on my fishing technique, though. It was so different from anything I'd ever experienced or read about that I crossed it off as one of those baffling exceptions that proved the rule. In fact, I didn't connect any of these experiences I've just described with each other although they all had one common denominator: in all cases trout had taken a fly on the surface that was moving in a highly un-Halfordian manner!

3

THE SUDDEN INCH

About this time, I began to suspect that I had been born in the wrong place at the wrong time. As surely as Don Quixote had been just too late for the golden age of chivalry, I had missed classic dry-fly fishing. But I still loved the sport, such as it was, and decided to salvage what I could from the brave—though certainly not better—new world I found around me.

I began rummaging around in the untidy attic of my memory, sifting through the experiences I described in the previous chapters, trying to find a solid starting point. My complete failure during the ultimate blue caddis hatch on the Beaver Kill that I mentioned at the beginning of this book didn't offer a clue. But how about that caddis experience on the Adirondack lake? Then, we had taken trout feeding on caddis and had taken them on the surface.

I dug out my longest trout rod, an eight-and-a-half-footer, and matched it with my lightest fly line. I tied up a level ix leader with two dropper attachments and put on three caddislike wet flies. This improvised rig was no joy to cast but it allowed me to cover fast-flowing pocket water quite efficiently when I worked in a downstream direction. In fact, I soon discovered that this technique was not only more productive than the usual upstream dry-fly method on this kind of water, but that it was more exciting, too. Fish slashed viciously at the dancing dropper, sometimes coming completely out of the water on the strike. And when I added the nineteenth-century wobble to the rod tip, making the dropper zigzag over these miniature, bubble-filled pools, results showed even further improvement. The two lower flies may have still hung dead in the current, but the top fly now bounced from side to side over the surface in a highly appetizing manner.

However, when I came to the end of the rapids where the water fanned out and flattened into a pool, results came to a standstill, too. There simply wasn't enough current to pull the line and flies away from me. Fish could see me from a greater distance in this calmer water, too. I was spooking every trout I approached long before I could dance my tantalizing fly over his head. I had added an exciting and effective technique to my fast-water strategy and one that I use often to this day, but I hadn't begun to solve the main problem.

It was in the slow water of the pools and flats where the main challenge lay. Here, sunk pupal imitations had been refused, skittered wet flies had drooped uselessly near my feet and conventional dry flies had gone begging. And it was precisely here where so many caddis hatched out and where I had seen so many plump, deliberate trout pluck the fluttering adults from the surface.

One tempting solution I had read about years before had been worked out by English poachers in an earlier and more caddis-oriented era. Two fishermen would position themselves on opposite sides of a slow but productive stretch of water after having tied their leaders together. They would then proceed very slowly upstream, holding their rods high so that only their dropper flies tickled the surface out in midstream. When a fish struck—and this must have been fairly frequently—one fisherman let out line while the other reeled the fish in. The technique was quickly outlawed, and I think rightly so, but you have to admire the ingenuity of it. Like the old, stillwater dropper technique, the poachers' dangling flies re-created the telltale motions of an adult caddis buzzing over the water surface.

The time-honored technique of dapping also occurred to me at about this stage. This is a stealthy way of taking trout without casting; the fly is simply lowered to the water's surface on a short line and dipped enticingly in and out of the surface film. I had watched professional French fishermen take lovely trout from the alder-tangled banks of the Tarn in the Cévennes Mountains with this presentation, but I couldn't pull it off on the wide-open pools of the main Catskill Rivers. You need concealment to get within dapping distance of your quarry.

One more approach that I'd observed in Europe seemed promising, though, and this was the Austrian method of fishing a caddis hatch which Hans Gebetstrauer, Fischmeister at Marienbrucke, had shown me on the River Traun. One evening after supper he took me out to the slow, wide flat above the weir—a place that was fifteen to twenty feet deep and that no one bothered with during the daytime. We stood on a small jetty and watched the water for several minutes and then, just as dusk began to fall, great clouds of caddis began to appear—as they did, I was told, on this section every summer evening. Soon every square yard of the surface was wrinkled with the rings of rising fish and it looked as if a flurry of hail had hit the water. The rises were gentle, though—no slashes, no boils, no way of telling in that half-light whether the fish were small dace or large trout.

Hans unwound a nine-foot leader from his hatband and replaced my leader with it. This prefabricated rig seemed heavy to me—it was certainly thicker than ix—and had one dropper fly tied in some three feet above the point. Both flies were standard British-style, downwinged caddis dry flies and seemed about size #14. I was instructed to cast this team directly across stream and to let the sluggish current take the flies slowly around until they had swung down directly below me.

It took an agonizingly long time for each cast to fish out, but if I tried to pick up prematurely to cover an especially promising looking rise in front of me, Hans gave a stern veto. Soon I could no longer follow my flies on the water, but the gentle "blip" sounds out in the darkness and the caddis flies bouncing off my face and crawling through my hair told me that the hatch and the rise were both still very much in progress.

Some time after I had lost all hope of ever getting a strike in this way, my line slowly went tight with that unmistakable authority you feel when a salmon pulls your wet fly. Then my reel began to give up line as the fish made its stately move up and across stream, steadily gathering speed. After I was well down into my backing, the line stopped moving and I started to apply pressure to regain some precious line, but there was no give at all on the other end, not even the telltale vibrations of a live but sulking fish. This stalemate continued for about a minute and then Hans took over the rod, felt the tension for a few moments, pointed the rod down the line and heaved. Something twanged out there in the darkness; then Hans reeled in rapidly, produced a small flashlight and began tying on another ready-made dry-fly rig.

"What happened?" I asked, somewhat unnerved.

"Wound around a boulder or a log," Hans answered. "Or both," he added for good measure.

I started casting out into the total darkness again and a few light years later my line once more went tight. Again a freight train moved off, this time even farther before it came to a stop. And again the rod ended up in the capable arms of Hans, only this time he reeled up and started to walk off the jetty.

"How big was that last one, Hans?"

"Who knows? The record is nearly eight kilos (over seventeen pounds!), but very few are landed in this place. Almost none of the big ones."

I believed every word he said and that gave me a sudden case of big-fish fever. "Can't we try for one more?"

"It is ten o'clock," said the voice of officialdom. "All fishing must now cease. Night fishing is strictly forbidden!"

I thought of asking him what we'd been doing for the past hour or more, but decided my broken German wasn't up to irony and followed him meekly back to the inn.

It had been an awe-inspiring evening, though, and I had hooked two huge trout fishing a dry caddis during a caddis hatch on still water. The method definitely deserved a fair trial on our home-water pools. I scaled down the leader dimensions before making my tests since I wasn't too worried about seventeen-pounders where I'd be fishing. Even so, the results were miserable: I had only two hits in three evenings of fishing. Apparently, this rather mechanical and unimaginative technique might hook two or three fish during a long evening on the Traun which literally teemed with trout, but it didn't begin to produce satisfactory action, even after dark, on our more sparsely populated waters.

Despite my so-far unsuccessful experiments, I still felt that the secret to the caddis presentation lay in manipulating the fly. My Adirondack experience and my more recent successes in the pocket water pointed to this, while the strictly imitationist approach of fishing using the realistic English caddis artificials with a free float had never produced more than a random fish.

It appeared to me that Halford had never come to serious grips with the caddis and a closer examination of his theory showed me why. Halford was a firm believer in "exact imitation": that he could create out of fur, feather and steel a replica of the natural insect so true to life that a trout couldn't tell the difference between the two. In his later books he concentrated more and more on refining the dressings for the best-known chalk stream mayflies, both males and females, duns and spinners. Did an Olive Dun flutter before finally taking to the air? Did a Jenny Spinner struggle before it died spread-eagled in the surface film? Did, for that matter, a Cinnamon Sedge skip along the surface while egg-laying? Halford simply wasn't interested. He was a portrait painter, not a newsreel cameraman.

These behavior-patterns, on the other hand, began to interest me more and more. Creating the telltale zigzag of an adult caddis bouncing over the surface of a slow pool seemed beyond the capabilities of my tackle and my skill. But perhaps there was some other easily recognizable caddis action that I could imitate. I resolved to spend less time fishing and more time observing in the future.

Like all good resolutions, this one was easier promised than kept. The most rewarding observations must always be made when flies are numerous and fish are feeding. Yet, despite notable lapses, my research eventually yielded two observations that I had never seen mentioned in either books or articles. First, evening flights of returning caddis invariably took an upstream direction. Very likely this is nature's way of assuring continuing populations in the headwaters since so many lumbering caddis larvae must be washed downstream during spates. Whatever the reason, this characteristic is pronounced and, as we shall see, significant. Second, both hatching caddis and the ones alighting on the surface for egglaying seemed to exhibit the same behavior pattern. They would float a few feet, then make a short, erratic lurch upcurrent—repeating this at intervals as long as they remained on the water. While these characteristics seemed far less dramatic than the zigzag flight pattern in the air, perhaps they would be equally distinctive to trout. After all, a fly actually on the water must be more worthwhile than a dozen in the air.

This small motion seemed well worth simulating and I was determined to try it out during my vacation in mid-June when the dark blue caddis hatch was in full swing. This fly, scientifically named *Psilotreta Frontalis*, is perhaps the single most abundant and important aquatic insect on the river I fish regularly. It begins hatching about Memorial Day and is seen in large numbers for an hour or more every clement evening until well into July. On cold, blustery days, it either appears earlier in the afternoon or makes no appearance at all. Unless I am mistaken, this is the caddis species that had baffled me on the Beaver Kill many years before. I decided to devote every evening for two weeks to settling this old score—whether I caught any fish or not. My hope was that a short motion of my fly in an upstream direction would convince the trout that the artificial was indeed a caddis.

In preparation for this test, I tied up some flies on light #16 hooks with dun tails, dun bodies and longish dun hackles. Not an exact imitation by a long shot, but it did give the impression of a blue caddis with its wings in motion and it had taken fish fairly well in fast, choppy water. More important, it floated high and tended to skitter instead of sinking when I twitched it. Trying this presentation in the usual up and across-stream manner was, as I had expected, no good at all. When the fly was twitched in this direction, it moved faster than the current and usually put a rising fish down. Fishing straight across-stream worked a bit better, but I still wasn't raising a very high percentage of the fish I'd spotted. Across and downstream? Heresy or no, I gave it a try and action picked up immediately. Later on, purely by accident, I threw a pronounced curve cast and this time when I imparted the minute twitch to the line, the fly moved a sudden inch straight upstream. Then, as it dropped back into a dead drift, it disappeared into the mouth of the best trout of the evening.

And now, for the first time, some of those baffling experiences from my earlier fishing days began to make sense. Those times when trout took only at the end of the float, just as the fly started to drag, were explained to a certain degree by the effectiveness of the twitch. And, I remembered now, the few strikes that had been produced by that technique I'd learned on the Traun had come just as the fly started to drag and not while it was skidding slowly and steadily across the current. Both situations had, it appeared, occasionally and accidentally created much the same effect on the water that my newly discovered caddis technique did.

I thought I had it solved right then and there. Cast across and a bit downstream with a good upstream curve in the line, landing the fly three feet or so above a noticed rise. Twitch the fly slightly upstream soon after it touches the water—before line and leader can start to sink. Then give it slack to float drag-free as far as possible. I was close, tantalizingly close, to the solution. In fact, everything was right—except the fly. In that calm, clear water, the silhouette just wasn't enough like a caddis. I was having a heyday with the small fish, but I wasn't fooling many of the better class of trout and this was indicative.

Sad as it may seem, all trout are not created equal. Rainbow trout, at least on our Eastern streams, are acrobatic but not very selective. Native brook trout will take almost anything when they're really on the feed. Freshly stocked trout of any kind tend to be pleasingly gullible. Wild brown trout, however, make few mistakes once they've grown up. When you're getting turn-downs from pound-plus browns you can be sure there's at least a small flaw in your technique.

What I now needed was a dry-fly imitation of the adult caddis that could stand the scrutiny of wary brown trout in glassy water. The most likely prototypes I could find were the English "sedges" that I'd used on the Traun and which are still being tied in Halford's style. These flies are tailless, have hackle at the head and longish wings tied of primary wing feathers and lying back over the body. I tied up several blue caddis on this model, making sure that the wings lay parallel to the body, covering it like an inverted boat.

This new fly looked very promising when I made a trial cast with it the following evening. The inverted V of the wings trapped a sizable air bubble, the fly rode the water in the precise attitude of the natural, and it looked just like the real thing to me. But when I started fishing it with my new technique a fatal flaw appeared. It just couldn't stand up to the rigors of the indispensable twitch. This small but decisive movement dislodged the air bubble and left the fly half submerged.

I was on the right track, though. On those few occasions when the fly didn't end up half-sunk, trout—and good ones—took it with confidence. I fished out the rest of the hatch that season with this imitation, working on my execution of the twitch to the point where I could bring the stunt off about ten percent of the time with this type of fly. It was demanding fishing, but results were far better than anything I'd known before.

The problem kept bothering me, though, because I felt I'd come so close to solving it. That winter as I sat at my vise tying up next season's supply, my thoughts kept returning to the caddis. What I needed was more floating power over the bend of the hook where some two-thirds of the metal lies and where there is the least amount of material that can take advantage of surface tension. Winding hackle the length of the body, as Halford had done in some cases, was tempting and logical, but it didn't work. There was some gain in floating power, but the bristle of hackle made the wing ride unrealistically, high above the body. Fore-and-aft construction—that is, with a hackle at the bend as well as at the head—caused the same winging problem and looked even less like the actual insect. After hours of frustration, I finally resorted to brute logic in an attempt to prove to myself that I had gone as far as I could go. The desperate syllogism went something like this: The bend of the hook needs the most flotation. Steely spade hackles from the throat of a fighting cock are the best-floating, most water-repellant feathers. Ergo: I must make the wing of spade hackle fibers. There was one hitch to this plan, though. Good spade hackles are nearly as scarce as hen's teeth and some otherwise superb hackle necks don't have any of these feathers at all. Exceptional necks may produce a dozen or so. In any event, these precious feathers must be hoarded for the tails of mayfly duns, as good flotation at the tail end is a critical problem with conventional flies, too.

After a lot of thought and experimentation, I finally came up with what I considered a likely looking fly. If I kept the body extremely thin, I found I could tie in the spade hackle fibers so that they would lie nearly parallel to the hook shank. Then, when I positioned small bunches of these along both sides of the hook shank and up over the top of it, a realistic caddis wing resulted. Finished off with two good hackles at the head, it looked very nearly as good as the Halford-type caddis when I floated the two side by side in the sink.

The next spring was a long time in coming—as it always seems to be—but finally I was on the river during a strong hatch of blue caddis. And for once abstract theory triumphed! The new fly floated perfectly even after it had been twitched, for the wing itself, which was twice as long as the body, acted as the floatingest tail a fly ever had. The silhouette seemed every bit as killing as the Halford-winged fly. And, for a bonus, the fly proved to be nearly indestructible—an unexpected but major blessing

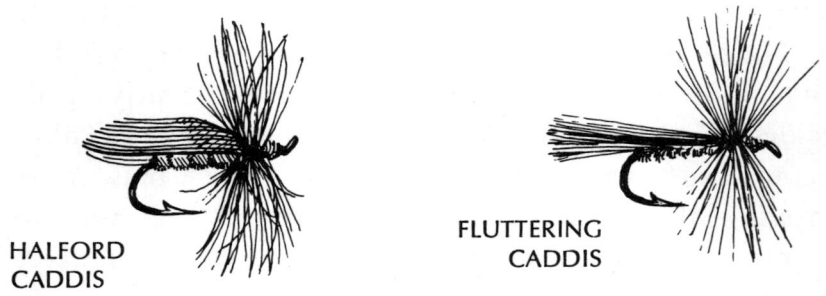

HALFORD
CADDIS

FLUTTERING
CADDIS

Dry-fly Caddis Imitations

since each fly carried enough spade hackle in its wing to tail a dozen standard duns!

The way in which trout take this type of fly puzzled me for years, though. They rise to it deliberately and boldly, seldom showing with the hurried slash which is so characteristic of their rise to the dapped dropper fly in fast water. I am now satisfied that the reason for this different type of take is the fact that more caddis are injured in hatching from the pupal sheath than ҫasual observation would indicate. We see many defective mayfly duns floating down the pool because their upright wings advertise their presence. The low-slung injured or dying caddis, however, easily escapes the angler's eye—though not the trout's. In any event, fish seem well acquainted with the adult caddis as a sitting duck once it has identified itself with that characteristic upstream lurch.

I have now used this type of caddis for several years and I can recommend the construction of this fly and the twitch-method of fishing it without reservation when caddis are hatching or buzzing over the water. I can honestly say that *I am now more confident of taking a good trout rising in flat water when the caddis is on than I am when fishing a standard dun during a mayfly hatch.*

This strong preference for fishing a caddis-fly hatch dates from a memorable evening near the end of that two-week June vacation and has been reinforced many times since then. A friend had invited me to fish with him on an especially interesting piece of water. The home pool on this stretch had been Theodore Gordon's favorite, according to Gordon's former fishing companion, Herman Christian. More recently, Hewitt had fished here regularly for decades often with LaBranche. Stepping into this water is like walking into Westminster Abbey. A piece of bad luck delayed me so that I didn't arrive till nearly dusk and as I joined my host at the head of this long, curving pool, I was further discouraged by his report on conditions. "It's pretty dead. A few flies in the air, but none seem to be hatching. The only real action I've seen was down under that overhanging hemlock." He pointed across and well downstream. "Several good ones rising there, but I couldn't get a touch out of them. I'm going to work this big variant up into the choppy water. Why don't you go down and give them a try? It will be dark in twenty minutes, anyway."

I walked down the bank and watched for a minute or two. There seemed to be six trout under the tree, rising at irregular intervals. The flies in the air were definitely caddis and I thought I recognized my old friend *Psilotreta*. I tied on a #14 dark dun imitation and went to work on the lowest fish. I will resist the temptation to file a cast-by-cast report on the subsequent fifteen minutes, but I do want to mention the final score: One fish raised and pricked; two hooked that finally kicked off; two wild yellow-bellied browns between twelve and fourteen inches landed and released. The sixth fish? I'm sure I sent him scurrying while playing number five which ran strongly upstream. A very respectable record, though, for a few minutes of fishing right behind one of the best anglers I know.

As I left that pool I couldn't help wondering what Gordon, Hewitt and LaBranche would have thought of my strange looking fly and the way that I'd fished it. Would they have disregarded it as they had the old dropper-fly technique? Or would they have given it a try themselves?

4

A SEARCHING FLY

My June vacation, that year, had been one of the most sat-
isfying fishing periods I'd ever known. It wasn't that the
fly hatches were bigger than usual or that there were any
more fish in the river. It was simply that I caught more
than in previous seasons and the apparent success of my
caddis experiments added excitement and drama.

But there's one flaw in every June: it eventually slips
into the doldrums of July. The river shrinks under the
high sun and drying winds. Currents that were once prime
feed lanes slacken or disappear. Hatches get sparser and
sparser. And unsuspected rocks, whitened with dead algae,
poke skull-like heads above the surface until it seems that
every day more living flesh is being stripped from the
river, exposing the bare bones.

This happens nearly every summer, of course. Yet I felt
the gradual deadening of the river more keenly this season
because of the red-letter days of the month before. Only
the sounds of feeding fish as I left the river after dark con-

vinced me that the trout hadn't deserted the river to school up in springholes and the mouths of brooks.

My caddis success seemed a small enough triumph now. The overshadowing problem was how to catch trout during the long lull of midsummer. Night fishing was, of course, one answer and yet I've never enjoyed fishing in pitch darkness.

One morning, when I was popping a fly into the few decent pockets left in a favorite rapids, I saw a good trout jump clear of the water halfway up the pool above. There, at least, was a sizable fish and a feeder. I decided to go up and work him over until I rose him or scared him back under the bank.

It had been easy to mark down his position precisely: he had showed under an overhanging hemlock branch that drooped down almost to the water. I walked up the shore till I was opposite his lie, then I waded out like an Indian to avoid sending out advance-warning waves. From a distance of thirty-five feet, I could see him clearly, poised near the surface and hovering nervously. Bright morning sun at my back showed him up so distinctly that I could count his spots, yet the same sun blinded him and I was sure he had no clue that I was there.

When I floated a #16 dun over his nose, his movements quickened, but he didn't rise. I cast again and again with a generous upstream curve to keep the 5x leader out of his sight. But the first chance at a fish like this is usually the telling one and after several presentations the fly didn't cause any reaction at all.

As I watched the surface, I could see no insects coming down river, yet the fish still seemed expectant. Then, above the surface, I noticed several small dark caddis flies boiling around in the shade of the overhanging branch.

Was this what had caused the leaping rise a few minutes before and still held his interest?

I tied on a small, dark, hackle-winged caddis and pitched it above the still-waiting fish. Again he fanned his fins in interest and even started to move toward the surface, but he refused at the last second. Again. And again. We played this game together for the better part of an hour and neither of us made a mistake. He never opened his mouth and I never botched a cast badly enough to put him down.

The cranelike stance I'd been holding was starting to tell in the small of my back so I inched ashore to shake out the kinks and enjoy a cigarette. My watch told me I still had a half hour till lunch so I decided to finish my smoke and give him one more try. Since I was fishing a caddis anyway, I would give it the telltale twitch this time even if it spooked him.

Ten minutes later I crept out into the water and made a few false casts to reestablish the range. Then I curved the same little caddis four feet above the fish and, after it had traveled a foot, I gave the rod tip a short, sharp, upward jerk, skittering the fly an inch upstream. I lowered the rod quickly to give slack and, as the fly proceeded down-current, the trout came up to meet it as if he were on tracks. He measured fourteen and one-half inches and weighed comfortably over a pound! I hated to admit to myself how long it had been since I'd taken a fish that good.

I quit while I was ahead and walked back to the house to write up the event in my fishing diary which had been neglected during the past fishless days. Recording the incident started me thinking, though. Had I just been lucky in finding a fish feeding actively on caddis? Or had I stumbled onto something bigger?

When the sun left the water at six o'clock, I was on the

river again. No fish were rising, but as this was a familiar stretch of water, I could concentrate on the best lies, passing up unproductive sections. And the twitched caddis raised—even took—more fish than I saw rise at random during the entire evening. Perhaps, just possibly, my new weapon was a dual purpose one—not only killing during a caddis hatch, but also a new way to pound up fish when none were rising!

The next few weekends were a revelation. I may not have been taking as many fish as I had in June, but I was enjoying distinctly good fishing—far, far better than the shrunken water had given me before.

Then, one evening in mid-August, my theory hit a major setback. I had driven upriver to fish with a friend and had left my box of caddis flies on my flytying table. A trip home and back would wipe out the evening, so I tied on a small, stiff-hackled variant, determined to muddle through as best I could. And, to my great horror, I still took fish. Not as many as I had been taking with the caddis, perhaps. But enough to make the evening a dismal success, for I had discovered, or thought I had, that the twitch was the important element and that my caddis was secondary—at least when this new presentation was used for prospecting.

The truth finally filtered through my disappointment, though. These trout hadn't been preoccupied with—or even expecting—caddis flies as they had been during the big June hatches. There wasn't a lot to eat during the drought days and fish were simply on the lookout for food in general. Under these conditions, any likely looking morsel was fair game—*once it had identified itself as a living insect.*

And *living*, I soon discovered, is the operative word. For it is motion that most often helps a trout separate the wheat from the chaff that the current brings his way. A bewildering variety of objects, both animal and vegetable, pass over a trout's window all day long in summer. Hold a yard of bellied-out cheese cloth in the tongue of a current for a few minutes some hot afternoon and you'll see what I mean. Along with the bees, wasps, houseflies, beetles, froghoppers, ants and aquatic insects that you'll strain out, you'll find at least an equal amount of small twigs, leaf cuttings, petals, berries, hemlock-needles and other debris nearly the same size, color and shape as the edible insects themselves. Trout can tell the difference, though, without studying entomology and botany. Insects wiggle, hemlock-needles don't.

Trout, especially wild trout, make this distinction between food and trash almost unerringly. I have tossed all sorts of likely looking objects to feeding trout from a carefully concealed position and had not more than one half-hearted strike in a hundred tries while that same trout rose, from time to time, to a wide variety of windfall insects. The trout I've been able to observe closely seem so discerning that it's a wonder they ever take our artificials.

What about those bits of leaves and twigs you so often find in trout stomachs? Don't let them mislead you. They're almost certainly pieces of caddis cases that have been separated by digestive juices. The same is true of the pebbles and grains of sand you come across when cleaning your fish. Caddis larvae, cases and all, are prime trout food despite their abrasive housing materials. And, I might add, not only do trout make few errors in selecting protein from random objects, but they quickly rectify their rare mistakes. If trout didn't eject foreign matter almost instantly, there would be no need to strike so quickly when fly fishing.

The many hours I have watched trout feeding on surface drift objects have led me to a theory on how a trout's primitive brain assesses information coming in from the eyes and triggers a rise. (Of course, this concept might make an animal behaviorist cringe, but it's a useful working analogy.) The mechanism seems like the three-tumbler combination lock on those wall safes which crooks are always cracking in B movies. Let's suppose, for illustration, that a trout has left his hiding place and is lying in a mild current, anticipating food. An object enters the upstream edge on his window and is judged to be the right *size* for food. The first tumbler drops and the trout's fins begin to quiver in readiness. More information comes in telling that this is the right *shape and color* to be food. The second tumbler drops and the trout starts his glide toward the surface. The object moves, indicating that it is *alive*. The last tumbler drops and the trout's mouth opens. I feel that short rises, or last minute refusals, are due usually to the fact that our flies fail to fulfill the third requirement and that the last tumbler in the trout's simple brain does not fall.

There are at least three more reasons why a twitched dry fly may produce a rise when a free-floating one will not. They may not, all three, be all-important all of the time, but they are well worth considering.

First, a twitched fly advertises itself. The hackle points denting the surface of the water are perhaps the artificial's greatest similarity to a living insect, whose legs cause much the same distortion in the surface tension. This is especially true when the fly lies outside the trout's upward-seeing window. Beyond this circular porthole, the under surface of the water looks like quicksilver. When a fly moves in this mirrorlike medium, it sends out sparkles that will capture a trout's attention—even at a considerable distance.

Second, a moving fly precipitates action. Most aquatic insects tend to take off from the water after a brief float —as trout know from many past experiences. Motion, then, telegraphs the urgent message of going, going . . . gone.

Third, trout are surprisingly rapacious. We rarely think of them as carnivorous because we usually see them daintily sipping insects from the surface. Thus, we tend to class them with the gentle warblers, flycatchers and swallows who share the same insects with them. This is a great mistake, for flies are meat as surely as are the minnows, shrimps, crawfish—even mice—on which large, so-called cannibal, trout feed. It is, therefore, highly likely that a fly, fluttering in distress, brings out the same predatory instinct that the flashing sides of a wounded minnow do—a stimulus usually strong enough to provoke an attack even from a fish already stuffed with food.

If you watch a pool carefully in a good light when only a very few insects are hatching, I think you'll come to the same conclusion about the attractiveness of a fly in motion. Especially on cool or rainy days when they can't take off quickly, flies will float down a hundred feet or more over the best lies in a pool, unmolested, only to be eaten when they make their first struggling attempts to fly. Yet only a few moments later, a fly of the same species that starts fluttering as soon as it hatches will be taken instantly by a fish that let the previous free floater pass by. In fact, this phenomenon is so striking that I am surprised it hasn't been mentioned more often in fishing literature. Which of the

above reasons is most important in explaining the appeal of
a fluttering fly, I couldn't begin to guess. Perhaps all three
of them are at work at the same time.

There's another interesting fact I've learned from watch-
ing a pool under these sparse hatch conditions. Trout will
often move five—even ten—feet to one side for an insect that's making a surface disturbance while they'll seldom swing more than a foot out of their feeding lane for a
quiet one. This long range attractiveness makes the
twitched dry fly an especially telling weapon for prospecting large, unfamiliar pools and it allows you to cover the
likely water nearly as quickly and efficiently as with the
old, across-and-down, wet-fly, presentation that's so effective in high water.

This added attractiveness of the fluttering dry fly becomes more important as the season advances and wanes.
During the bursting days of spring, when water levels are
optimum and hatches are at their peak, classic dry-fly technique often gives a good account of itself. But once summer, low-water levels have set in conditions change dramatically. After the first of June on Eastern streams and
rivers, the most common situation the fly-fisher faces is the
"nonhatch." A few flies may struggle to the surface at
choice times of day, but there will seldom be enough of
them to make fish rise regularly or create a marked preference for any specific size or pattern. If you want to catch
good trout in any numbers at this time of year, you must
become a prospector rather than a hatch matcher. Under
these conditions—and they usually dominate the greater
part of the open season—trout must be goaded into rising to the surface. The fluttering dry fly becomes the most
successful tactic.

A further advantage in using this technique for prospecting is that it allows you to catch trout out of more of the water more of the time. With today's crowded stream conditions, this is invaluable. Long, slow sections of pools or flats are usually avoided by fishermen until dusk during the summer months while pockets, runs and heads of pools seem to absorb most of the pounding. I've had pool after pool all to myself for hours as early as June since I discovered the twitch can be productive in slow water during most of the day.

Let's suppose it's five o'clock on a summer afternoon and you've come to a pool three to four hundred feet long, seventy feet wide, curving slightly to your left as you face downstream. Very likely, there'll be a fisherman working the pockets in the riffle above and another stationed at the head of the pool where the current tongue flows in. The rest of the pool is yours, though, and the fish in this part have probably not been molested for several hours. This is a fairly representative situation on our larger, Eastern streams and it is made to order for the style of fishing I've been describing.

The best tactic, in this case, would be to get on the left bank, which is the weak side of the current, and walk downstream a courteous distance below the head-of-the-pool fisherman. Your polaroids will tell you that the deepest section of the pool is two-thirds of the way across-stream toward the outside of the pool's curve and that the thread of the current follows this deeper trough. This fifteen- to twenty-foot wide section will almost always contain the most interesting fish at this time of day for it has both the deep holding and hiding places plus the main, food-bearing flow.

There's no need to make major changes in tackle to fish the twitch presentation here. A size #14 or #16 hackle-winged caddis is ideal, but if you don't have one a size #16 variant will do. If the latter has very long hackles you may have to clip some fibers off the bottom to keep it from flipping onto its head when it's twitched, but this is minor surgery. There's no need to tie up special leaders, either. One of 3x is about right for a size #14 fly and 4x for a #16 is as fine as you'll need to go. Your leader will always be pointing directly away from the fish and a 7x tippet would be an affectation here that would hamper your presentation and snap far too easily. A standard, nine-foot length is all you'll need too, for the end of your fly line will also be a long way from any interested trout.

Step quietly into this pool, now, and only far enough in to clear your backcast and to put you within easy range of the prime holding water. Cast your fly about ten to twenty degrees downstream from straight across so that it falls on the near edge of the deepish water with the line and leader curving upstream, if possible. Keep your rod tip high as you finish the cast and, within a second after your fly hits the water, raise your rod sharply so that the fly darts upstream about an inch. Then, lower your tip a bit to give slack and feed out extra line through the guides by wobbling your rod.

This maneuver should give you six to eight feet of drag-free float. A fish that has been attracted by the seemingly alive offering may take at any time during this period. Then, as the line comes tight and the fly starts to skitter across-stream toward you, be especially alert, for this second motion often precipitates a rise from a hesitant trout.

All this time, it's a good idea to hold your rod at an angle of about forty-five degrees above the horizontal to cushion the leader in case you are caught off guard by a striking fish. Remember, your line and leader are constantly tightening in this kind of presentation and any respectable fish can easily snap even a 3x leader if your rod can't give with the sudden strain. Then, too, a slightly high rod tip keeps several more feet of line belly off the water and helps to give you a more drag-free float.

After your fly has started to drag visibly for six or twelve inches at the bottom of the float, give a sharp jerk on the line with your left, or line-holding, hand to pop the fly quietly under the surface. You can learn to do this with a minimum of disturbance quite quickly and it is important to the success of this technique. A fly skittered all the way across the pool and then upstream on your pickup creates a wake that can needlessly alarm fish lying below or to one side of the water you have just covered; whereas a sunk fly is far less disturbing. Admittedly, your fly won't float cockily quite as long if you subject it to these periodic dunkings, but this is glassy water and you must use extra caution or you'll spook the fish before your fly covers them.

After you have recovered the extra line, lift it gently off the water and dry the fly thoroughly with several brisk false casts before dropping it across stream again—this time five to six feet beyond the first cast. Fish this cast out in precisely the same way you did the first one and then place your third cast several feet farther across-stream than the second one.

Three, or at most four, casts should cover any taking fish in that twenty-foot-wide, eight-foot-long section. You should then wade cautiously eight or ten feet directly down-current and make the same series of across-stream casts. Repeat this pattern until you have reached the bottom part of the pool where the water gets too shallow for likely fishing this early in the day.

If you proceed carefully, you will be surprised to find

DEEPER WATER

Prospecting down a pool

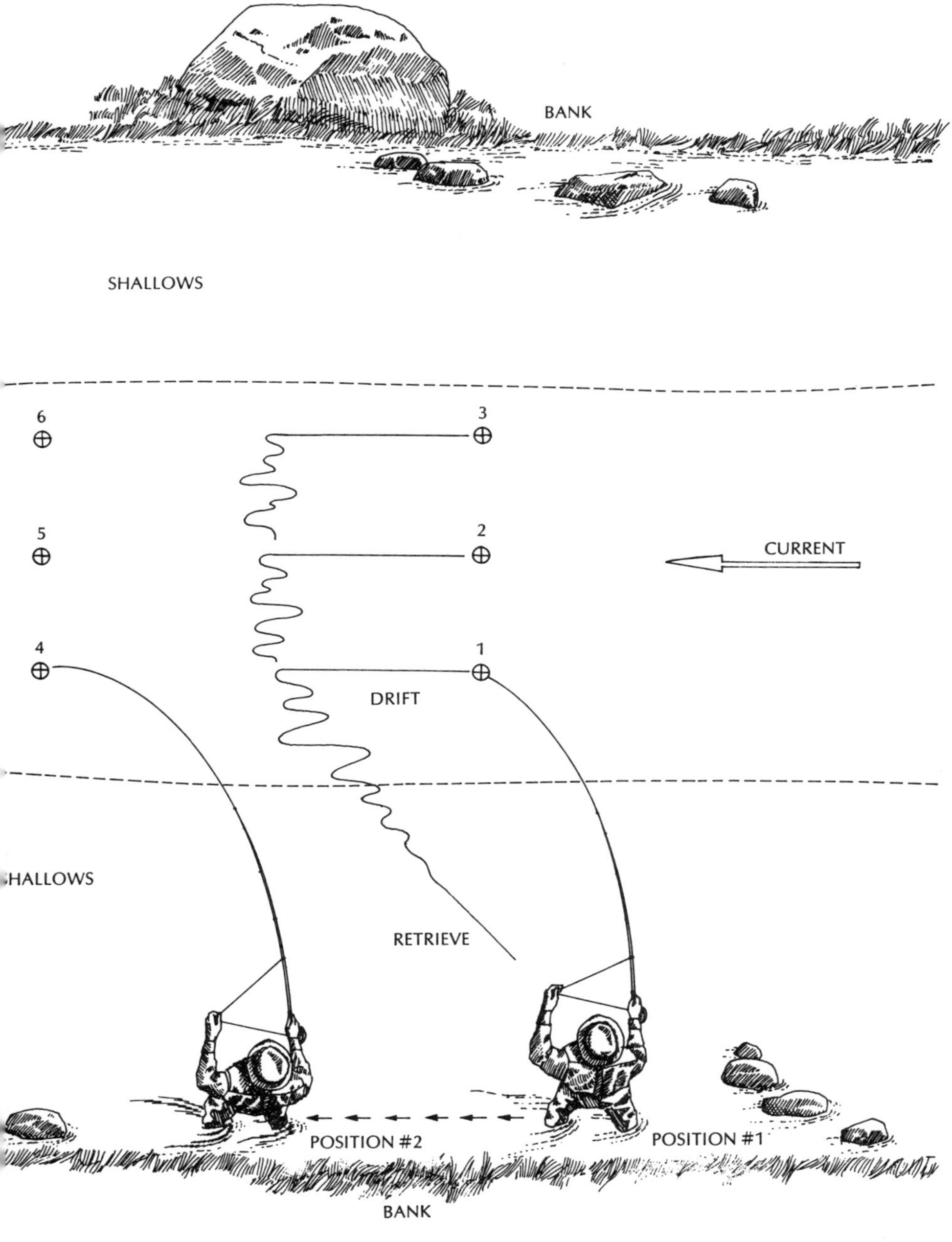

BANK

SHALLOWS

6
⊕

3
⊕

5
⊕

2
⊕

CURRENT

4
⊕

1
⊕

DRIFT

SHALLOWS

RETRIEVE

POSITION #2

POSITION #1

BANK

with the fluttering dry fly

how many fish you can raise in this manner even when there's no indication of surface feeding. And at least 150 feet of the productive part of a pool can be covered in twenty minutes or so. You might expect a lot of splashy, short rises when using a tantalizing technique like this, but such is rarely the case unless the area is inhabited by small brook trout which have the annoying habit of false-rising, anyway. In fact, I've found that when a decent-sized trout comes to a fly fished in this manner, the take is usually quite businesslike.

I have also noticed that the fewer the random rises you see in a pool and the deeper it is, the more necessary it is to use the twitch to raise fish. Trout may rise fairly often in two feet of water for a free-floating fly, but to induce them to come up three-or-more feet when they aren't making regular trips for insects, seems to call for this extra stimulus.

The need to induce rises was particularly noticeable last season on the river I fish regularly. Near the end of the previous summer, we had suffered an Act-of-God flood—the highest water in some twenty-five years. Whole generations of aquatic insects were nearly wiped out and the hatches were less than a quarter of what we've come to expect. With this scarcity of flies and free-rising fish, I resorted to the twitch more and more often as the season advanced and I found myself using it some evenings even at dusk, when fish can usually be expected to rise freely. It would have been a sorry season indeed if I hadn't relied on this technique, for time and again a free-floating fly would be ignored by a fish I'd marked down, and then the twitch would raise him on the very first cast.

In fact, I've discovered the twitch is a valuable ace-in-the-hole in almost any situation. Even in fast water, and

even when there is heavy surface feeding, it has proved itself effective as a last resort on fish I have failed to take
with the standard presentation. Nowadays, when I find I
can't raise a good fish that I see feeding actively, I always
make a twitch presentation from across-stream and slightly
above him before I move on. This tactic has worked so
often that I am sometimes tempted to make this presentation my standard one and give up the drag-free, upstream
delivery altogether!

5

TIGHT CORNERS

The long, curving pool I described in the previous chapter was, admittedly, made to order for twitch fishing a dry fly with an across and downstream presentation. There's plenty of room for your backcast; you can keep well to one side of the fish and the slow, smooth water makes it easy for you to stay in touch with your fly and manipulate it. Fortunately, such stretches are very common on our larger trout streams.

But, you're probably wondering, what about brooks? Aren't there many more miles of narrow trout waters than there are of broad ones? And how can this wide open style of fishing help you catch trout when you're hemmed in by trees or bushes? The answer is, of course, that it can't, but there are variations of this technique that can produce *the same effect with the fly on the water*—even though the actual delivery is quite different.

There's one small tributary brook that I fish quite often where the twitch pays off handsomely for me; in fact, according to my records, it regularly outproduces the conventional upstream method. I have proved this to my own satisfaction many times by fishing upstream for half a mile, resting the water awhile, then fishing back down again. Whether I run this informal test in the morning or in the afternoon, the result is always the same: I catch more and better fish on my return, even though many fish must have been alarmed on my upward trip. This brook averages only six to eight feet wide and, like most mountain streams, has many short, round plunge-pools and no long, deep flats. Nowhere is the water over a dozen feet wide and it is bordered tightly on both sides by mature trees, making an across-stream presentation, which might be possible on a small meadow stream, absolutely out of the question.

When you leave a main river to fish a feeder stream like this one, both you and the trout you are pursuing have entered a different world. Temperatures are more constant up here nearer to the springs where the water is shaded from the heat of the sun. This means that both the food supply and the feeding activity will be spread out more evenly, with several varieties of flies hatching out sporadically in ones and twos during most of the day while there is seldom that last-minute flurry just at dusk you can expect on the main river.

Here the trout's enemies are quite different and his defenses are drawn up accordingly. On the open river, danger comes mainly from above in the form of ospreys, herons and kingfishers. Depth alone offers security from these attacks and even the slim cover provided by surface ripples or a small overhanging branch can make the trout feel secure. None of these tactics will do on small brooks where raccoons and mink are the major predators. Depth is of little use against a pursuing mink and it is seldom available in brooks, anyway. Safety here means an undercut bank, a muskrat hole or a slot far under a rock. The good fish will stay close to—even inside—these makeshift strongholds and dart out from time to time to take whatever likely food the current brings their way. They are seldom selective, therefore, and rarely will one of these fish glide up under your fly and drift back with it for a closer examination. These are sudden, opportunistic fish that will either lunge at your fly or ignore it completely. And perhaps this is why the twitch is so effective here: it can trigger a rise from an otherwise indifferent trout.

Equally important to you is the restriction of the arena. You are now in confined quarters and funnelled into a vertical plan of attack from either directly below or above. There are compensations, though, for if you are limited in space so are the trout. Their few good lies stand out clearly and you need waste little time in random prospecting.

There's often a bigger reward than your catch in this type of fishing, and that's the beauty and the intimacy of the setting. For these steep hillsides usually have discouraged the logger and the farmer. As a result, many brooks still flow pure and cool through tight banks under tall shading trees. A Frenchman I met while trout fishing in Spain described this setting perfectly. Though he seemed well beyond spawning age, he said with obvious relish, "It's like fishing in a boudoir!"

As you have probably suspected by now, this type of water must be twitch-fished almost directly downstream. There appear to be two problems attached to this: how to keep the trout from seeing you as you approach from

above and how to keep from alarming them when you retrieve the fly upstream after a presentation.

If you have fished a stretch of brook upstream first, or if
you have fished the water before, you will know the places
with the depth and cover to hold worthwhile fish. If not,
you will have to proceed more slowly, trusting to what
your polaroid glasses tell you. In either case, you will have
to proceed in approximately the same manner, and this is
the technique that I have found most productive.

Let's suppose, now, that below you lies a miniature falls
and, under that, a pool barely longer than it is wide—the
top quarter of which is filled with bubbles while the rest is
clear though streamy. You have approached to within
twenty feet of the head of this pool, are on the left bank
facing downstream and standing next to a large tree trunk.
If you have moved into this position slowly, taking care to
keep low, there's every reason to believe that the fish
below haven't seen you. Resist temptation: don't stand out
in the middle of the narrow arcade formed by the trees in
order to give yourself extra casting room. It is far better to
use the background cover provided by trees or bushes
along the bank and to creep a little closer to the pool if
you can. Check behind you carefully, now, to be sure your
short backcast has a clear path, then cast downstream to
where the white water ends on the near side of this small
pool. Whenever possible, it's a good idea to drape your
casting line over a convenient boulder so that it won't be
caught up in the fast chute above the falls.

Within a second after your fly alights, impart the twitch
and then give all the slack you can. Your fly will now either drift down toward the lower rim of the pool or, if
there is a countereddy, it will swing off to your side of the

pool and start back up toward the bubble-filled section at the head. In either case, your fly will soon start to drag severely and, if no take has occurred, you will be faced with the problem of getting it back out of there quickly and quietly before its wake alarms the fish.

The best way to do this is to swing your rod tip sharply in toward your own bank and retrieve the fly gently up the near edge of the pool or even along the shore itself, depending on the ruggedness of the terrain. Once the fly is out of the pool proper, you are set to cast again. A word of caution here, though. If you retrieve your fly across the cobbles, do so very gingerly and, even so, it pays to check your hook point after fishing each pool.

Your next cast should be delivered to the upper center of the pool, and this time it will almost certainly float straight downstream after it has been twitched. Again, swing the fly quickly but gently toward your bank after it starts to drag badly and retrieve it up the near side of the pool which has already been fished over. The third cast should be made to the far side of the pool, though again to the head of it, and if no fish has been raised after this presentation, you may be fairly sure you're not going to score in this particular spot and you should proceed downstream to the next likely place. Go quietly now, and keep a close watch. Darting shadows may reveal feeding and holding positions of trout in the pool and this information should be kept in mind the next time you fish here.

All this may sound like very quick work, but, if done properly, it takes more time than it seems. Your approach should be carefully planned and so should the intended path of your backcast. It's equally important to figure out how to drape your casting line across a rock or exactly where it should lie on the water to prevent your fly from being snatched away immediately and drowned before you can fish it. In working a pool of this size, your fly may be on the water in a fish-taking position for only five or ten seconds while the whole operation, if executed thoughtfully and properly, may well take that many minutes.

The pool I have just described actually exists. Even though it is very much like other good pools on this brook, it became my favorite because for several years a polished, snag-free log lay across the head of it suspended about two feet off the water. This held the line conveniently out of the current and made a perfect presentation almost absurdly easy. When it went out in the flood of 1969, I felt as if I'd lost an old friend. But, knowing from those easy experiences that this place always holds an especially good trout, I have spent many hours working out a substitute presentation. I now take advantage of some conveniently placed rocks to support the intervening fly line on the first two presentations. Then I have to sneak over to the opposite bank and make a backhand delivery to cover the far side of the pool on my third cast. There's a lesson in this: few lies on a brook like this are impossible if you think, plan and practice enough.

Of course, you can fish water like this with the wet-fly dropper technique. This can be just as effective if executed properly, but there are two possible drawbacks. One is that the currents in these miniature pools are seldom strong enough in midsummer low water to pull the flies away from you vigorously. This means that you won't be able to stay far enough away from the fish. The other is that to fish this dropper method most efficiently you should use specialized tackle—a long rod and very light line— and this will handicap you if you plan to return to the main river later on to catch the evening rise.

RAPIDS

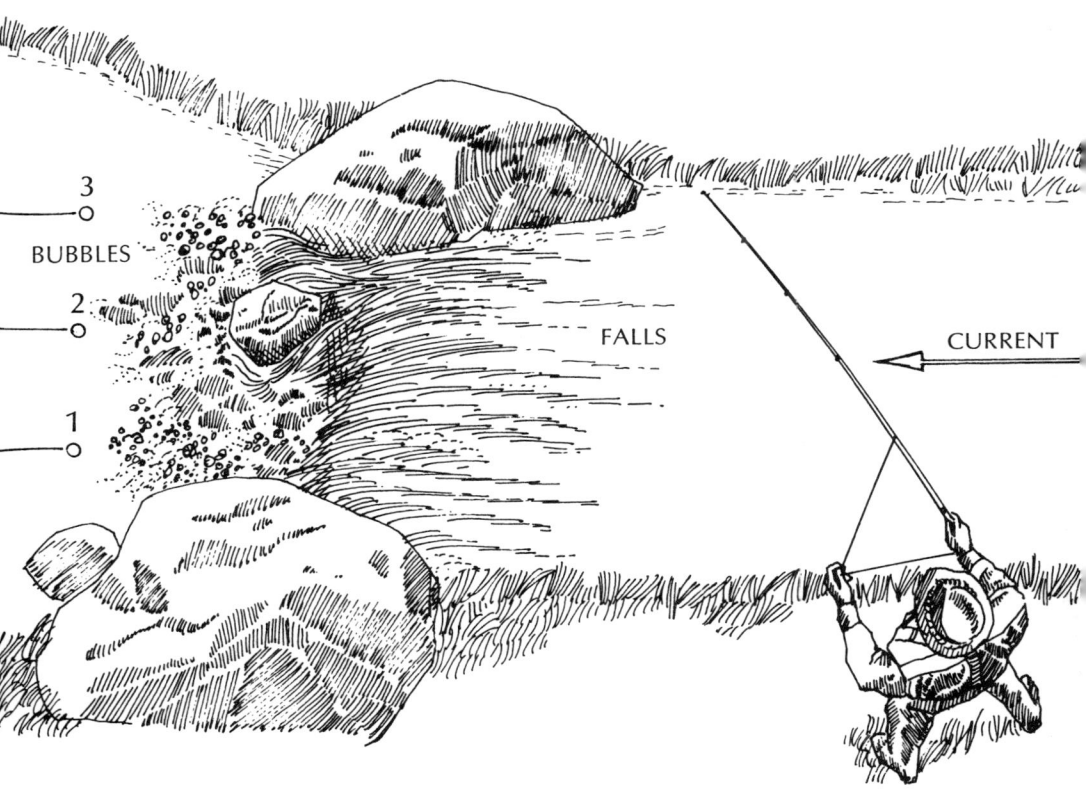

3

BUBBLES

2

1

FALLS

CURRENT

Prospecting a small pocket-pool

In any event, I think there are at least two reasons to explain why I catch more trout in small brooks on the dry fly while I'm working downstream. The first is the added attraction of the twitch itself. The second equally important reason is that drag often works for you when fishing down-current, while it almost always hurts you when fishing upstream. In the latter case, faster currents at the exits of these pocket-pools rip your fly off the slower water above, making the fly race out of the small pool much faster than the prevailing current. Not only will fish usually refuse a fly behaving in this manner, but they will also very often flee in terror from it. On the other hand, when fishing downstream, a dragging fly moves slower than the stream and seems to stutter up-current. This creates an excellent imitation of a struggling or hatching insect, and many fish are taken by happy accident when some drag that you hadn't figured on has set in.

I should add here that pocket water on larger streams can also be fished effectively in this same manner. These miniature pools on large waters have much the same characteristics that the short, bank-to-bank pools of brooks do, and a downstream presentation here offers the same advantages for identical reasons. A further benefit is that the downstream method is far less fatiguing. The rapid-fire casting required to pop your dry fly in and out of a pocket from a downstream position can weary your arm in a few minutes if you do it properly. This is also, incidentally, punishing to your rod. Chan Young of Naponoch, New York, who is the most skillful and dedicated upstream pocket-water fisherman I have ever known, has to have his excellent two-piece bamboo rod referruled every year for this very reason. I wonder why he doesn't have acute bursitis as well.

There are some situations, even on wide rivers, where snags or obstructions prevent casting to a fish from the side and from above. For two years now, an eight-inch thick, thirty-foot-long maple has been leaning out into a favorite pool of mine while its roots have remained anchored in the bank. This makes a choice holding spot for trout, which drop back a few feet downstream from the protecting branches when they're in a mood to feed. The only possible presentation to them is from below. When one of these fish refuses a free-floating fly repeatedly, it will sometimes succumb to a delicate variation of the twitch.

This minor tactic is accomplished by positioning myself as far across-stream as possible—which usually means casting up to the fish at about a forty-five degree angle. The fly is then delivered as near as possible to the overhanging branches. After the fly alights, I try to give it a minute twitch—not enough actually to move the fly, but enough to rock it slightly so that the hackles twinkle in the surface tension. Here it is best to underdo it. If the fly lurches downstream in this glassy water you are almost sure to send the fish scampering back under the branches. However, if the fly doesn't budge at all, you have just another drag-free float over the fish and nothing—except a few seconds of your time—has been lost. It's hard to pull this stunt off more than one time in four, but if you err on the gentle side, you'll execute it perfectly within a few casts. This succeeds in inducing a take often enough to be well worth a try before moving on.

There's still another variation of this technique that appeals to me, partly I guess, because of the sheer laziness of it. You can't use this method in many places, but where conditions are just right, it's a pure joy. Some slightly curving pools or flats have only a narrow band of likely fish-holding water while the rest of the area looks relatively barren. This is usually caused by a rock ledge, a cut bank or a deep trench on the outside curve of the pool which concentrates all the best lies into a narrow slot.

When I reach a place like this, I grease most of my leader as well as my line and tie on a freshly oiled fly for maximum flotation. Then, starting at the head of this stretch, I cast my fly across and slightly downstream into the fish-holding ribbon of water and start wading gently downstream with the current, just keeping pace with my fly. Every six or eight feet, I impart a slight twitch or jiggle to the fly, and I proceed down the pool until the drag gets too severe or the fly gets soggy. At this point, but only then, a new cast must be made back into the slow current-tongue. In some places I can cover nearly a hundred feet very effectively in this manner without recasting. The fishing is so effortless and so much fun that I wish nature had constructed more water exactly like this.

In all types of fishing I've described in this chapter, you can use either a suitable variant or a hackle-winged caddis —both of which will float and stand up to the twitch quite well. The caddis, however, is far better if you have one. There are several reasons for this. The silhouette of the caddis represents many more types of flies than the variant does. It looks a lot more like the many land-bred insects, for instance, when viewed from below and it makes a passing imitation of a stone fly—an insect type that becomes noticeably more common when you fish up feeder brooks. It is also far easier to cast, for it offers much less frontal area and therefore less wind resistance. Lastly, it is easier to present under almost all conditions because it strikes the water sooner. With a variant, your line and leader may often have started to drag well downstream before your fly has finally fluttered down to the surface. The more streamlined caddis, however, can be made to hit the water at the same moment your line and leader do. This gives you time to twitch the fly and get some productive float before the inevitable major drag sets in and ends the usefulness of that presentation.

There's one last situation that calls for a downstream presentation whether on large streams or small. This is when trout are feeding at the bottom lip of a pool where the water gathers speed before rushing into the rapids below. Often, you will find fish rising quietly here at dusk, though seldom at other times of day, for this is one of the trout's favorite feeding stations when taking spinners or spent mayflies.

If you try to cover these fish from below, you will face the same obstacle you did on the small brook pool: the fast chute of water between you and the trout tends to whisk your line away before your fly even hits the water. The ideal presentation here is from across-stream and slightly above the fish, again with your line and leader curving upstream, if possible. In this way, your fly will cover these wary feeders before the leader comes into view and your fly won't start to drag until it is well past the fish and into the rapids below. However, do *not* twitch the fly when fishing under these conditions; the reasons for this are covered in the next chapter.

6

WHEN DEAD DRIFT IS DEAD RIGHT

While I now have no doubt that a dry fly, twitched properly is by far the most effective presentation during a caddis hatch and that this method offers the best results for random prospecting when few fish are rising, I would look both foolish and fanatical if I disregarded the special situations when conventional dead drift is far superior. One of these times is when trout are feeding on spent mayflies or spinners. Since many trout fishing books deal with this subject only in general terms, I think it's worth a closer look.

All mayflies go through a second metamorphosis after they have reached the winged state. It is in this clearer, more glossy form—often confusingly different from their dun appearance—that they return to the river from the grass and bushes to mate and die. Probably the best-known example is the Coffin Fly which is the funereal black-and-white spinner form of the well-known Green Drake. But every mayfly goes through a similar transformation and their spent forms, too, end up on the water and are eaten by trout.

This mating and dying process usually occurs at dusk. Admittedly, some early-season flies return to the river during midafternoon, or even earlier. But I have seldom found that the fish feed on them to any extent, probably because the more nourishing duns have just hatched out or are still hatching out at this time of day. My own experience has been that spinners become really important to trout only during the food-short days of summer and that from mid-June on, a good rise of trout to these spent flies occurs just as the light begins to fail.

I used to refer to this magic time of day as "the duffer's half hour" because it often seemed that every fish in the river would start rising at nightfall, but I have long since dropped the term as all too often this can be a frustrating and fishless period. Lord Grey of Fallodon describes it perfectly: "The *look* of the evening rise is so often the best of it. Numbers of trout appear to be rising frequently and steadily and confidently, but when the angler puts them to the test, they disappoint him. On some evenings the trout cease to rise after an artificial fly has once been floated over them; on others they continue to rise freely, but will take nothing artificial, and the angler exhausts himself in efforts and changes of fly, working harder and more rapidly as he becomes conscious of the approaching end of the day."

Spinners are usually the quarry during this type of feeding. I think there are three reasons why fish take them so eagerly at this time of day, despite the fact that spent mayflies may be less nutritious than some other food insects. Unless fresh flies are hatching out on the water at the same time, spinners are usually by far the most abundant food available during late summer evenings. Then, too, after the sun is off the water, it cools down and returns to the trout's optimum metabolic range which gives fish an inner drive to feed. Lastly, as darkness falls, trout feel more secure and will take up feeding stations near the surface or in the shallows for easier topwater feeding where they would never venture in full daylight.

The usual tip-off to the spinner-feeding situation is the trout's position in the pools and the type of rise they make. Both of these will be covered at greater length in a later chapter on rise-forms. But, for our purposes here, trout rising gently and fairly regularly in the bottom half of a long quiet pool at dusk should lead you to suspect spinners. The fact that you can't see any flies in the air nor any on the water shouldn't make you change your premise. On the contrary, this is strong supporting evidence; caddis or duns, the other two most likely causes of a rise, would be clearly visible on this glassy water while the spread-eagled spinners floating flush in the surface film can seldom be seen unless they float right past your waders. Hovering midges are always another possibility, but larger trout seldom feed on these with any regularity and, when they do, rises are either leaps or slashes.

I wasn't fully aware of the importance of spinners nor of the trout's frequent preoccupation with them until a July evening several years ago. Six good trout were lined up in a weak current thread of a favorite pool, feeding regularly, yet I couldn't get a touch. Suspecting midges, I put on a dark #20 fly with some difficulty in the gathering darkness and tried again, but received only a few short rises for my efforts. Since it was now too dark to change flies again, I gave up fishing for research. I pulled out a yard of cheesecloth, which I usually keep in the pouch of my fishing vest, and waded out into the hip-deep water where the fish had been rising to strain a sample from the current. Specks soon appeared in my improvised net, but as it was too dark now for any identification, I carefully rolled up the cloth for further examination in the full light of the kitchen sink.

What I discovered were dozens of spinners of two varieties—both with glassy, transparent wings. One had a rusty-brown body and was about size #16; the other was a bit smaller and had an olive body. Where they had come from in such numbers, and what their dun forms had looked like, completely baffled me for I had seen no hatches of comparable flies in recent weeks. I have since come to the conclusion that duns often hatch out after dark and that some spinners we find belong to species that fishermen are otherwise unfamiliar with.

At any rate, I tied up some flush-floating imitations and had one on the end of my 5x leader well before dark the following evening, and was waiting patiently for the line-astern formation of trout to start feeding again. Up they came at about the same time and I caught two and hooked another on the brown-bodied imitation before the disturbance of playing the fish put the survivors down. I now tie on a spinner imitation quite regularly as my last fly of the evening. Since I have found this highly productive, I will pass on to you the method of fishing it that I have found most effective.

First, there is little use in prospecting with this type of fly and at this time of day. Fish either start taking spinners or they don't and you will seldom induce a take with this imitation. When you see the signs of fish rising to spinners, you should try to get across and slightly above a regularly rising trout and tie on an appropriate artificial. This, admittedly, is not as easy as matching a hatch of duns which are easier to see and to capture, but you may be guided by

the flies you have seen dancing up and down over the riffles earlier in the afternoon or by specimens you may have
captured during recent outings.

Cast your fly now, three to four feet above the rise-
form of the fish you are stalking, preferably with an upstream curve in your line and leader, so that the fly will be
seen first. Strive for an absolutely drag-free presentation
with this delivery, *and this is critical*, for these flies are either dead or dying and any motion on their part would
seem unnatural to the trout. By their lazy and confident
style of rising, the fish will confirm that they, too, expect
to find these flies immobilized in the surface film and that
they are not in the least worried about the fly of their
choice escaping. This is fortunate for the fly-fisher since
these lightly-dressed, flush-floating artificials will sink
through the surface-film, instantly, if you so much as jiggle
them.

If you have chosen a suitable fly and have presented it
naturally, you're likely to see a small, dimpling rise near to
where you suppose your fly to be. (I use the word "suppose" advisedly, because you can seldom see a flush-floating fly in this half-light more than ten feet away and you
should be thirty feet or more from the fish in this smooth
water.) Now is the time to exert self-control: do not rip
your line through this still water with a sudden, violent
strike. Heavyhandedness is not necessary here, anyway.
For a trout takes a spinner with confidence and a slow,
steady tightening of the line will set the hook if, indeed,
the fish has taken your fly. If, on the other hand, he has
merely risen to a natural nearby, the gentle pull on your
line will not create a slashing wake that might put the fish
down. You may well take him on the next try.

If you hurry this sort of fishing or undertake it with a

feeling of desperation—that this is a last-minute chance to fill your creel after a disappointing day—you will almost surely be disappointed. This is a time to work for one good fish, or possibly two. Approach this last half-hour of the day resolved to make your mark with the best fish you see feeding, and you will leave the river with that feeling of contentment fishing is supposed to give you.

Personally, I find this fishing fascinating and the only problem is the guesswork involved in picking the right fly —although there seems to be a good deal more latitude in this type of fishing and in this poor light than there is when matching a fly to a natural dun. Experience from previous days and from other years is often a good enough guide, although I am quick to take samples with my tucked-away cheesecloth if I seem to be drawing a blank.

Perhaps the charm, to me at least, of this situation is explained by my early trout-fishing expectations. There is no form of fly fishing I encounter on Northeast rivers, regularly, that comes as close to pure Halfordian conditions as this does. First I mark down a regularly rising fish. Then I tie on what I consider to be the best imitation of the natural insect. Finally, I cast this fly onto slow, clear, demanding water and let it float drag-free over the known lie of a fish. Halford himself couldn't have asked for more. Since I enjoy this sport for a half hour or more on most evenings for some three months of the season, I can now excuse the sparse—and getting sparser—dun hatches of late April and May that disappoint me so often. Spinner fishing, as I now practice it, is as near to chalk stream fishing as I ever expect to find on my local rivers, and though fishing time per day may be short, it is nonetheless sweet.

Occasionally, land-bred insects—especially flying ants and jassids or leafhoppers—cause much the same feeding patterns that spinners do and in the same long, slow stretches of the river. Usually, however, this will occur much earlier in the day, most often in midafternoon, when full daylight can help you identify the exact insect trout are taking. These small terrestrials also float flush in the water and are so entrapped in the rubbery surface film that they are almost incapable of movement. Because of this, and because the artificials must be very sparsely dressed, the same spinner presentation should be used in this case. Only your fly needs to be changed.

Grasshoppers, on the other hand, are not only large and strong, but they seem to be especially annoyed by finding themselves on the water and they protest vigorously as they float downstream. Therefore, it is a good idea to twitch an imitation hopper quite decisively as it approaches the lie of a waiting trout.

Occasionally, very occasionally, I happen to be on the right river at the right time to witness a hatch of duns that is of sufficient density and duration to start trout feeding in the classic manner. When I meet these conditions I always start fishing up and across-stream with a dead drift presentation of the best imitation I can muster. At times like these, I bless Halford's great contribution to the sport and agree with him wholeheartedly that this is the peak of trout fishing. I firmly believe that in Hampshire during the late nineteenth century, before road washing and insecticides had started to take their toll even there, big hatches (which occur occasionally to this day on the Test and the Itchen) were the rule rather than the exception. What marvelous years those must have been on the richest of all rivers when such a theory could have been conceived and demonstrated.

I've found it takes profuse and prolonged hatches, which

are rare in North America, to psychologically "imprint" trout to the point where they will start feeding selectively on one species of insect, intercepting individuals at regular intervals and accepting an imitation solely on the basis of color and size. Even so, the twitch or—better still, with a conventionally dressed dun—jiggle technique must sometimes be used, even under these optimum conditions, to take an especially good trout. Perhaps this is because the slightest motion calls attention to my fly in the midst of a fleet of naturals or because even the best of imitations may appear to be a crude replica to an experienced and suspicious trout. When I have failed to rise a regularly-feeding trout after a dozen casts in the conventional manner, I now move upstream and try him with the presentation I've described often in this book. In this situation I try to make my dun—which is far easier to sink than a hackle-winged caddis or a variant—just twinkle in the surface film two or three feet above the trout or barely outside his window.

I must admit, though, that I have found this trick is hard to pull off with very small flies—size #18 and smaller —because they're hard to see and to keep in touch with at any distance. Fortunately, small naturals seem to be less active than the larger ones and if trout are coming all the way up to the surface to take a tiny insect, they will usually come up for an imitation, too. However, I find that a slight twitch can sometimes make the difference even with midge-sized flies, and I have used it with some success when light conditions have made it practical.

There's one other important insect that I have passed over so far and that is the stone fly. It is less interesting to the fly-fisher than the mayfly and the caddis fly because most species are sporadic hatchers and most seem to crawl out of the water to transform themselves into the winged state, thus escaping the trout's notice. A few, though, do hatch out in large flushes on the water surface and they are well worth considering. One of these is the early-season "salmon fly" which appears in clouds on some Western rivers. Unfortunately, I have never fished one of these rivers when this was occurring, but I should think that an effective dry-fly imitation of this huge stone fly must be hard to create, hard to cast and hard to float. There are, however, several species that hatch out on the water in good numbers on Eastern streams. I will have to limit my personal observations to these.

Two of these stone flies I have always found disappointing: one has a bright yellow, and the other a green body. Both are about size #14 and appear in large numbers on May mornings on the rivers I fish. Both, too, are obliging enough to hatch out on the water's surface, but for some reason—perhaps they have a bitter taste—trout will have nothing to do with either of them. I have never seen one taken nor have I ever found one in the stomach of a trout!

There's another stone fly of about the same size that hatches out a few weeks earlier, and this one the trout seem to relish: the Early Brown Stone or *Taeniopteryx fasciata*. Preston Jennings in his *Book of Trout Flies* and Art Flick in the *Streamside Guide* have covered this stonefly with some detail. I have little to add since I, too, have found that an imitation fished just under the surface beats the dry fly during this hatch. However, if I ever do come up with a killing dry imitation, I will surely fish it with the twitch as I've noticed that these flies hop around on the surface actively before they manage to take off in the cold April air.

Perhaps you're wondering, at this point, if trout prefer this insect in its prehatching or "wet" form, isn't this true of many other insects? And wouldn't this make wet-fly fishing more productive than the dry fly? And, if this is true, why am I devoting nearly all of this book to the surface-fished fly? These are all good questions. I think I have good answers.

7

WHY DRY?

There are probably more misconceptions about dry-fly fishing than there are about any other form of sport. Many think that the floating fly is more sporting—that it embodies a nobler ideal—than the sunk fly. Others admire the purist as a man who imposes an artificial limitation on himself to conserve the dwindling stocks of trout. While both of these theories may flatter the dry-fly man, I can't agree with either of them. I use the dry fly the majority of the time because I've found it is distinctly more effective on the rivers I fish during most—though not all—of the season.

This statement may seem absurd to anglers who are familiar with stomach-contents studies showing that some 90 percent of the trout's food is taken from beneath the surface. I don't question the accuracy of these figures for a moment. My point is that there is just no way for a flowing-water fisherman to imitate the great bulk of this food. For most caddis-in-case are picked off while they are stationary on the bottom; most mayfly nymphs are taken as they crawl slowly across a stone. And how can you re-create these behavior patterns with fly-fishing tackle in running water?

Chalk streams or stable limestone streams are possible exceptions, for most of these waters grow a rich pasturage of weed beds which harbor large populations of swimming-type mayfly nymphs and fresh-water shrimps. Both of these creatures can swim rapidly when disturbed or when changing location, and this behavior can be imitated easily with the sunk fly. But rain-fed, freestone rivers—and these are the great majority in North America—contain mostly crawling or clambering types of mayfly nymphs and the turtlelike caddis, neither of which lends itself to conventional nymph imitation except during those brief moments just prior to hatching.

The still-water, sunk-fly fisherman, on the other hand, is easily able to duplicate this slow-moving portion of the trout's diet, for his line and lure are not continuously washed away with uncharacteristic haste. In fact, one of the deadliest pond-fishing techniques imitates the slow progress of a nymph, larva, shrimp, crawfish or whatever across the bottom and it seems to work even when trout are not actually feeding. I was introduced to this method years ago on the headwaters of the Gunnison in Colorado and I have never seen a surer way of taking trout in still, shallow water.

One day about noon on the Taylor River, which is the Gunnison's parent stream, I made the acquaintance of a local fisherman who asked me if I wanted to try some really different fishing. When I admitted I was game, he led the way up a steep hillside following the course of a small trickle of spring water. After a half mile of laborious climbing, we came out into a nearly level area of mixed meadow and aspens that was littered with beaver cuttings. When my breath and my pulse finally returned to normal —we were up over eight thousand feet by now—I crept over to the nearest beaver pond to see what all the climbing was about. I couldn't see a fish or even a rise anywhere, but right in the center of this half-acre pond was a dark patch which I supposed was made up of debris and rotting leaves. I made a perfunctory cast out toward the middle anyway, to show I was a good sport, and the instant my line hit the water the brown patch fractured into a hundred moving pieces! Not only was this small pond paved with trout, but a few of them appeared to be as big as three or four pounds.

After I'd exercised the trout thoroughly with several futile casts, my companion came up and showed me the battle plan. He cast a wet fly out into the deepest part of the water, put his rod down on the beaver dam and then led me a couple of hundred yards uphill to a second pond where he told me to do exactly as he had done. We took our time getting back to the first pond and, as we came near, he made his approach on hands and knees while I stood back. From his hidden position below the dam, he started to retrieve his line, just inching it in, and in a few seconds he was into a sixteen-inch trout.

We repeated this process for several hours, allowing about fifteen minutes for each circuit, and took or hooked a trout every time. The trick was simple: the trout couldn't see us and didn't notice the transparent leader lying on the bottom. While this method seemed to have more in common with ice-fishing than with fly-fishing, each retrieve held a moment of high excitement— especially with those few large trout out there. For some reason, though, the one- to two-pounders always beat their betters to the fly, but we caught enough of this size to keep any angler happy.

All this was happening, mind you, under a bright, midafternoon sun without a ripple on the water and, although we never saw a sign of a fish feeding, the trout found this presentation irresistible no matter how often we repeated it. It's probably just as well that this method is impossible on running water as our streams and rivers are depleted rapidly enough as it is!

So much for the exceptions, though, interesting as they may be. The fact remains that most of the trout's food on most of our rivers is picked up off the bottom and there's little the trout-fisher can do to imitate it. The middle portion of the water—anywhere below the surface and above the gravel, where sunk flies most often travel—is almost devoid of food after the first flushes of spring are over.

As far as fly-fishers are concerned, trout seasons can be divided into three distinct parts. The main factors involved are water level and water temperature and, although there is usually a correlation between the two, water temperature is the more important influence.

During the first weeks following opening day, you can be sure that streams will be running high and thermometer readings will be low. Fish metabolisms will also be low which means that trout will feed sparingly and their actions will be sluggish. Under these conditions, you can't expect fish to dart up toward the surface for flies or passing bits of food. Your offerings must pass close to the trout's holding position near the bottom of the stream if you are to have any chance for success.

This first lean period lasts for two or three weeks in

most Northeastern states and the fly-fisher must imitate the bait-fisher's tactics if he wants to catch even a fish or two. Large wet flies and nymphs or streamers and bucktails are the most productive lures. Sinking lines are used by most veteran early-season anglers, but some achieve the same results on smaller waters by casting weighted flies up-current and allowing them to sink deep as they drift back on a slack line.

The second period begins when flies start to hatch out on the surface after lunch, during the heat of the day. With the exception of some low-lying, spring-fed streams, this seldom occurs much before May 1. The critical water temperature that ushers in this sort of fishing seems to be forty-five degrees. Flies rarely hatch out when the water is colder and even this temperature brings no assurance of surface-feeding action.

Now, fly-fishing has truly begun and for the next four or five weeks you can expect the best fly hatches of the season. Floating lines are the order of the day now. Wet flies and nymphs, fished just under the surface are taken eagerly by trout and, of course, dry-fly fishing is at its peak of popularity.

This feast for fish and fishermen usually comes to an end all too soon. Shortly after Memorial Day hatches begin to dwindle—except, perhaps, for occasional flurries just at dusk. At this time of the year, water temperatures will hit the high-sixties or low-seventies in the afternoon and water levels shrink to summer lows.

The third fishing period has now begun and, with the exception of brief spates and short spells of cool weather, low-water summer fishing can be expected from now till the end of the season. These conditions will prevail for the next three or four months—a full two-thirds of the average season—or for the greater part of the dedicated trouter's stream-days. With rare exceptions, dry-fly fishing will be by far the most effective tactic—mainly because most of the available, imitatable trout-food will now be on the surface or in the surface film.

With the exception of those few minutes on summer evenings when aquatic insects rise up through the water to hatch out, the surface film is the main conveyor of food. I have proved this to my own satisfaction time and again by taking samples with the yard of cheesecloth I keep tucked away in the bellows of my fishing vest. When I skim a surface sample with this in midsummer—even in the morning—I find an interesting collection of insect food. But when I make a second test from below-water, allowing the surface film to flow unchecked over the top of my improvised net, I trap nothing, or very little, in my mesh. Old fishing writers called the surface the "crust" of the water and I admire their crisp description of this strong, rubbery layer. The term may be an understatement, though. My simple research seems to indicate that the surface film is more like a rich, thick frosting on a very thin cake!

Many trout fishermen may find it hard to believe that the surface and the very bottom hold nearly all of the food most of the time because they desert the streams to fish lakes, salmon rivers or the ocean after the first few weeks of the season and don't experience the prolonged low-water conditions that dominate our Eastern rivers all summer long. But the water-supply people will, unhappily, confirm my estimate of summer river volumes and I have no doubt that low-water net samples taken by other anglers will parallel mine.

Actually, there's one obvious reason why most insect

food is on the surface during the summer. Insects tend to float. And, with legs or wings outstretched, they get hopelessly caught in the elastic surface tension whether they are alive, dying or dead. In the high waters of early spring, many flies get churned under in the riffles or pockets, but under drought conditions currents are gentler, and most insects either ride through on top or soon bob back to the surface.

Trout must instinctively know that surface film is an important source of food and this must condition their feeding reflexes. I have no doubt that trout in all but the fastest-water lies concentrate their attention upward during most of the season toward this endless belt of food passing over their heads.

These long periods of low water exert another important influence, too. As the water gets lower, rivers flow slower—much slower—and this, in turn, effects the feeding habits of trout. You may have noticed that many more fish rise in the leisurely parts of the river than in the rapid sections. One reason for this may be simple metabolic efficiency: it takes less energy to make a round trip to the surface in slow water than it does in fast. But I think there's an even more important factor at work here. There's good evidence that the *longer* a fly stays in view, the *stronger* the stimulus it exerts.

I had no idea how influential this element of speed-of-travel was on surface activity until I started feeding experiments on wild trout a few years ago. This project began as an attempt to supplement the diet of trout during the food-short summer months, but it delivered an unexpected bonus as a study of trout-feeding behavior as well.

The food I selected was *lights*—a butcher's term for lungs—which is about the only type of meat that can still be bought at a reasonably low cost. Since this is a spongy material, it floats and you can watch the trout rise to it as they feed. It is also the only available food I have found that wild trout will take readily. I have never been able to induce river-bred trout to take any of the commercial pellets, floating or sinking, but wild or unstocked trout will feed on lights greedily the very first time it passes over them.

My plan was to feed each pool on Sunday night after I finished fishing it. I would wade out into the riffle at the head of a pool and scatter two or three pounds of lights that had been run through a hamburger machine and then watch the action in the pool below me for a few minutes. These small bits of meat separate quickly in the water and, as they float downstream by the thousands, create a "hatch," artificially, that is seldom rivaled by the naturals.

It wasn't long, though, before I noticed an interesting phenomenon: the heaviest and steadiest rising occurred in the slower, bottom two-thirds of the pools while far fewer trout rose in the faster currents at the top. This surprised me because fishing results had led me to believe that the greatest concentrations of fish lay where the incoming riffle flattened out near the head of the pool. But the significance of this didn't strike me till one night later that season when I fed the stream after a three or four-inch rise in water. This evening was warm, clear and ideal for trout feeding as the results of my own fishing up until a few minutes earlier had proved. Yet, surprisingly, my offer of manna produced very little surface action though I knew the pool was well stocked with trout.

This pattern has repeated itself so many times since then that I now only feed when the water is truly low. But it pointed up a parallel situation about natural surface feeding that I'd overlooked for years: I'd always seen more random rises in slow water than in fast and more in low water than in high. This, of course, is not always the case during heavy hatches, but I said "random rises" and by this I mean fish rising opportunistically to odd insects. The increased distance to the surface—a matter of a very few inches —doesn't appear to be the deterrent. It is far more likely, as I said earlier, that the trout is induced to rise more strongly the longer an item of food remains in view. This attracting period certainly lasts longer when currents are slow.

There are at least two more reasons for the superiority of the dry fly in low water that deserve mention. One, that I mentioned earlier, is that a dry fly—even when floating naturally, but especially when twitched—advertises itself better than a wet fly. The other is that a dry fly is veiled in mystery: trout don't get a clear look at its fraudulence because of the distortion the many hackle points create in the surface tension while the imperfections of a sunk fly stand out nakedly to the fishes' eyes.

All the statements I have made about the amount of food in the surface film and about the greater effectiveness of the dry fly apply mainly to the low-water conditions which dominate most of our season. Rivers swollen by early spring run-off or sudden summer spates are quite another matter. Under these conditions I have found that the wet fly or nymph will outfish the dry fly most of the time, except perhaps, during a heavy hatch of insects.

Even though this book bears a dry-fly label, there may be lessons dry-fly men can learn from the many centuries of successful wet-fly fishing. Perhaps it will be worth our while to examine, briefly, what this practice has been like.

8

WET-FLY LESSONS

Fishing with the artificial fly is an ancient art; it is described in written records as far back as the third century A.D. and there is no evidence that it was a novelty even then. Dry-fly fishing, which is not one-twentieth as old, developed out of, and owes a great debt to, the rich and practical folk-tradition of wet-fly fishing.

In the beginning, and up until about a century ago, all flies were wet, incapable of floating. The main reason for this was probably metallurgical—strong, light-wire hooks that could be floated by hackle had to wait for modern alloys and tempering· processes. But despite this and other technological disadvantages, early fly-fishers dressed killing artificials and presented them to the fish with deadly effectiveness.

There is no mistaking what the earliest flies were meant to imitate—they are clearly painstaking attempts to duplicate specific insects and this is central to the early tradition of fly-fishing. Nondescripts, gaudy attractors and silver-bodied fancies which might be mistaken for small minnows or fry, are much later developments. Aelian, writing less than three centuries after the birth of Christ, tells how the Macedonians tied red wool and wax-colored cock's hackles on their hooks to imitate a fly called the "Hippurus" when they angled for the spotted fish in their streams. And, when fly-fishing emerges again after a long literary gap, in *The Treatise of Fishing with an Angle* during the mid-fifteenth century, we find this imitationist heritage is still strong and thriving. In spite of vague tying instructions given in *The Treatise*, the twelve recommended flies are all recognizable as imitations of common aquatic insects, and twentieth-century experts John Waller Hills and G. E. M. Skues both felt they could match each artificial with its corresponding species.

These flies, with their dubbed-fur bodies and soft-fibred wings, were so effective that they may have been accepted as the standard patterns for several centuries. Izaac Walton, writing some two hundred years later, lists the same dressings as his "Jury" of twelve flies to "condemn all the trouts in the river" and recommends capturing a specimen of the fly on which trout are feeding and matching it with one of these artificials. Yet, as deadly and realistic as they may have been, these flies were not asked to fool trout strictly on their own merits. They were almost always given an added dimension of life through manipulation by the angler.

It is important to remember, here, that there was nothing effete about this folk tradition: early fishermen copied natural insects and fished with these artificials only because the technique worked. There was no hint of affectation or posturing in their sport. They fished the worm and minnow lovingly and unabashedly when conditions dictated, as their writings clearly show. The sole aim of the exercise was to catch lots of trout, and generations of anglers had found that imitation insects produced more fish most of the time.

The presentation of these flies was also practical and businesslike and the method was surprisingly versatile considering the tackle of the day. Rods were long, five to six yards long, and an equal length of horsehair line was tied to the tips of them. This gave the angler at least a thirty-foot range—enough, perhaps, for most small stream conditions yet; even so, Walton cautioned his pupil to stand back from the bank and to "be still moving your fly upon the water."

Those words "moving" and "upon" are especially significant, for Walton goes on to advise that, whenever possible, only the fly and none of the single horsehair leader should touch the water. Gathered together, these hints tell us that the artificial was often played upon the surface. Walton's disciple, Charles Cotton, has given us such a detailed description of dapping with a live insect that we can be almost certain that the imitations were fished in this manner, too. With a fifteen- to eighteen-foot rod, a fly could be bounced on top of the water at a range of over twenty feet easily and effectively while the angler camouflaged himself in the shrubs and bushes on the bank.

Of course, these flies were also fished sunk, in the conventional across and downstream manner. Cotton's insistence that wings should be set equally and evenly so that a fly would swim properly in the current certainly bears this out. So, even though the apparatus used may have been cumbersome and primitive by our standards, the result with the fly in or on the water was both varied and realistic.

All this began to change, though, some hundred years after Cotton's time. When the use of the reel became popular, both line and casting range could be lengthened at will and shorter, more wieldy rods came into style. This may have been a great step forward in convenience, but the dapping or surface-fishing capabilities had to suffer. For the next half century, anglers concentrated on sunk-fly tactics and refinements soon appeared in this area.

Upstream wet-fly fishing in fast water was one of the most important of the new methods and W. C. Stewart was its eloquent and influential apostle. Here, with the fly drifting back freely toward the angler, manipulation was out of the question. However, Stewart, well grounded in the folk tradition, still insisted that the trout must be "deceived by an appearance of life" and recommended a type of artificial that might seem to have a life of its own. In *The Practical Angler*, published in 1857, he specified long, soft hen-hackles that would wiggle and play in the current turbulence and thus give the illusion of aliveness.

Sunk-fly technique was, at this point, nearly complete as we practice it today. But the surface-fished fly, except perhaps for some dapping on small overgrown brooks, had disappeared from the running water repertoire for over a hundred years. No wonder then that the dry fly burst upon the scene some thirty years after Stewart's time with an impact from which the fishing world hasn't recovered to this day.

Halford's dry-fly influence broadened our sporting possibilities in many ways. A. H. E. Wood's greased-line, wet-fly technique—a method in which drag is avoided or greatly reduced—and the Hewitt-LaBranche dry-fly system have enriched our salmon fishing and both owe a great debt to Halford. But in the trout-fishing area, Halford may have imposed artificial limitations along with his dry-fly contribution—whether he intended this or not.

For, while he restored the vital surface-fishing element of the old folk tradition, Halford overlooked another and perhaps equally important aspect. All the early fly-fishers had insisted that their flies, like Halford's, duplicate the naturals as closely as possible, but they went one step further. They tried to duplicate the *behavior* of live insects as well and they did this in three main ways. One method was the surface dap and the dancing dropper fly. The second was by swimming the fly under the water and across or against the current flow. And, lastly, there was Stewart's softly dressed fly with its sinuous hackle and built-in motion. All three performed handsomely under the appropriate conditions.

But Halford's dry fly, though it was presented with Stewart's upstream delivery, couldn't have moving, breathing fibers, for the stiff cock's hackle which kept the fly afloat had no motion of its own. For the first time in fishing history, the imitation fly was truly on its own: it now had to dupe the trout solely on the basis of its size, shape and color.

So powerful was Halford's dead-drift, imitationist doctrine that it has not only dominated dry-fly fishing to this day, but it also revolutionized sunk-fly fishing for a number of years. Skues' upstream, dead-drift nymph technique was almost precisely the same idea as Halford's except that his fly was an inch or so lower in the water. Skues also fished a famous chalk stream in Southern England (until he was asked to resign his rod privilege for fishing the sunk fly!) and he was equally opposed to the indiscriminate flogging of a river in the hope of taking an unseen fish. His imitations were as scrupulous copies of the underwater naturals he'd collected as were Halford's of their top-water forms. Yet these two men waged the bitterest and most publicized battle in the history of angling over this minute difference. Never was a fisherman more admired and followed than Halford. And never was a disciple more sternly rebuked than Skues!

Skues says he adopted the drag-free presentation because he was convinced that nymphs lay inert for quite a while just under the surface before hatching out. Whether this opinion was due to accurate observation or to Halford's dogma, or both, is still subject to debate. The fact is that the most common chalk-stream nymphs are of the swimming type, very active in their daily routine, and their behavior is easy to imitate with rod manipulation during most of the periods when trout feed on them. Why Skues turned his back on this wide-open opportunity to take trout, whether they were feeding visibly or not, must have been for Halford's ethical—almost moral—reasons!

When transplanted to this country and popularized by E. R. Hewitt, the dead-drift nymph technique seems even more artificial. Most of the nymphs in Hewitt's water were of the clambering or crawling variety and these very definitely do *not* lie doggo just under the surface before hatching out. One of them in particular, *Iron* (*Epeorus*) *Pleuralis*, commonly called the Quill Gordon, hatches out under the surface and pops up through the overhead layers of water as a winged insect. Other fast-water nymphs that I have observed hurry to the surface and hatch out as quickly as possible. If you have any doubts about this, watch a trout taking emerging nymphs near the head of a pool during a hatch. There are no leisurely, self-assured takes here as there are with the sure-thing spinners in the evening. Trout are extremely active when nymphing in running water and you can be sure they're expending this extra energy only because their quarry is in the habit of escaping scot-free if they aren't quick off the mark.

Caddis-fly pupae—particularly those inhabiting fast water—are especially agile swimmers as they rise to the surface to hatch. Entomology books leave no doubts about this and neither do the trout which make sudden and vigorous rushes when taking emerging caddis. Even so, they miss their quarry so often that a winged insect flying up from a subsurface boil is usually the first clue in diagnosing a caddis hatch. In my experience, fishing a pupal or nymphal imitation upstream and letting it drift back naturally is the *least effective* method of taking trout from beneath the surface during a good hatch of either type of insect.

Apparently, English fishermen are coming to the same conclusion because the dead-drift nymph is going into eclipse across the Atlantic on all but the most sacred chalk streams. Today, the "induced take" is causing far more discussion and the technique is well worth trying on our waters when working on an individual fish or prospecting a choice lie. Cast your nymph well above the fish in a generally across-stream direction and, when you judge that the fly is approaching the trout, tighten the line so that the artificial will start to rise and swing. This sudden upward motion duplicates the behavior of a hatching or escaping nymph and will often precipitate a take when other methods have failed.

One of America's greatest wet-fly fishermen, James Leisenring, recommended a technique very much like this for taking large, difficult trout. He felt that the ultimate presentation was to make your wet-fly nymph rise up through the water with a fluttering motion just in front of the trout's nose. This can be done even in very fast water with a slight variation of the English "induced take." I have used this killing presentation many times. Start out by getting well above your fish and casting slightly to one side of it to make sure you have the range exactly. Then cast directly toward the fish, stopping your rod near the vertical position with a tug so that the line will jump back toward you and fall in a series of slack curves. Your nymph will now sink as it drifts downstream, but, as the line comes tight, it will rise suddenly to the surface right in front of the trout's lie. Only the wariest or sleepiest trout can resist!

Whether this presentation works because it brings out the cat-and-mouse instinct of the predatory trout or simply because it makes the artificial more alive is a question for the animal behaviorists. I do know that it produces handsomely, as do other moving-fly techniques, even when fish seem to be off their feed.

Perhaps we all make too much of the distinction between the wet and the dry fly. For centuries there was only one type of fly and it was fished on or under the surface depending on where the trout were feeding. Fishing the sunk fly in a drag-free manner had a brief, though recent, vogue and is again becoming a "minor tactic" as Skues so modestly labeled this method when he launched it in 1910. But what about the surface-fished fly? Dry-fly cultists have always insisted on a drag-free presentation, yet their voice is also a rather recent one. During most of its history, the top-water fly has been danced, dapped or manipulated in a lively manner and only recently has it been called upon to sail serenely downstream like an object of art. Which of the two surface methods is the "minor tactic"? Years from now, perhaps, we may have the perspective to answer that question.

9

THE HIDDEN HAND

It may appear, at this point, that I am flying in the face of every known authority and recommending that the dry fly should be fished with drag. But if you analyze the technique that I've described you will see that this is not the case. Let me illustrate this point with a parallel from another sport.

I remember the first sports-car race I ever witnessed and my amazement at the way the cars "drifted" around sharp turns nearly sideways. After the race I was introduced to one of the drivers and I asked him, "What's the difference between a 'drift' and a 'skid'?" He looked puzzled, as if I'd asked him to describe the technique of mouth-breathing, "Well," he said finally, "a skid is a drift that's out of control." Then he added for good measure, "And I guess a drift is a skid that's under control."

And that's exactly it. A dragging fly is a presentation that's out of control and the method I've described is a moving fly that's very much under control. Carefully calculated and limited manipulation is a far cry from drag.

The unnatural appearance of a dragging dry fly is usually compounded because dry flies are traditionally fished in an upstream direction. This means that when the hidden hand of an intervening current begins to pluck the fly off course in a steady and therefore uninsectlike manner, it hurries the fly down-current as well. The first motion may be unrealistic enough to discourage a fish from rising, but the second is often enough to send a trout scurrying for shelter—especially if the drag is pronounced enough to make the fly furrow the water.

Wet-fly fishermen seem less worried about drag and, in fact, seldom use the word although they pay close attention to the speed of travel and the underwater route of their fly. The classic across and downstream delivery virtually guarantees that the fly will be dragging during the entire presentation from a dry-fly man's point of view, and yet it is one of the most consistently effective wet-fly casts. This seems like a direct refutation of the dry-fly man's no-drag doctrine, but there are important differences between the two techniques.

In the first place, the wet fly travels under the surface and leaves no alarming wake. Then too, since the delivery is made in a generally downstream direction, the imitation will be fishing slower, instead of faster, than the current flow. This is one point on which the many schools of sunk-fly fishers seem to agree: a wet fly or nymph traveling faster than the current is doomed to failure except, perhaps, under nearly still-water conditions.

The wet fly cast in this manner will also be moving across-current, which would be unnatural for a dry fly, but not necessarily so for a subsurface imitation. Many forms of underwater life—swimming nymphs, shrimps, small crawfish and fry—often move in this manner while insects on the surface have a distinctly different behavior pattern. This fact was brought home to me after a running battle of several days with a particularly good trout on the lower Tarn River in France. The fish lived in the slack water just inside a tunnel in the overhanging alders. A fast current swept past the entrance to his lair and every time I popped the fly into his feeding spot it was snatched away briskly. The fish was impossible to reach from above or below and there wasn't room for a curve cast in that narrow slot. Finally I tossed him a nymph from my across-stream position. He chased it out and took in the fast water four feet below the entrance to his feeding place. What he mistook that nymph for I'll never know, but he was far more broadminded about the underwater behavior of food than he was about surface offerings.

Perhaps the wet fly calls attention to itself by swimming counter to the current. Certainly it separates itself from the many bits of flotsam in the current and declares itself to be alive and edible by its motion. Probably the dragging wet fly is highly effective for all these reasons. It accounts for more fish than the dead-drift sunk fly—especially when the water is high or the current is strong.

The dry-fly fisherman has no such license since he is presenting an imitation of top-water food. He must do everything in his power to avoid drag and there are four basic ways in which he can do this. As most of these well-known methods play a large part in the success of the twitched fly, it might be a good idea to review them at this time.

The simplest and oldest technique for avoiding drag is accomplished by keeping as much line as possible off the water. Dapping is this method carried to the Nth degree.

However, since ability to keep line off the water is mainly a result of your choice of tackle, I'll reserve a full discussion of this for a later chapter.

Another method, and one which is especially useful for long deliveries across tricky current-tongues, is the wavy S line presentation. To make this cast, check the follow-through on your final forward delivery and wobble the rod-tip strongly before the line falls to the water. This lays the line out in a slack, serpentlike pattern and the S's will have to be straightened out before the current can pull your fly off course. The S is a valuable presentation under many conditions, including a straight-downstream delivery, but it has one major drawback as far as our new technique is concerned. There is so much slack in your line that you are out of touch with your fly for some time and, therefore, have little chance to deliver the indispensable twitch at the critical moment.

Mending the line after it has fallen to the water is a drag-reducing maneuver that is a favorite with salmon fishermen although trouters, especially wet-fly experts, use it from time to time, too. In this case, part of the line is lifted or flipped off the water and rolled, usually upstream, into a curve to cushion the damaging effects of an intervening current-tongue. This can be repeated as often as is necessary until the cast is fished out. The salmon angler tries to accomplish this without disturbing the drift of his wet fly. It is even more important that the dry-fly man mends his line without jerking his fly across the water or he may well put down the fish he is casting to.

A modified mend is often useful when a strong current flows near the angler's position. The harmful effects of this flow can be delayed by throwing a loop up-current at the last moment, just before the line falls to the water. All you have to do to accomplish this is to make a pronounced up-stream motion with your rod and arm as you finish your forward cast. Many anglers do this unconsciously, but if you're not one of them it's well worth remembering and practicing.

The most important method of avoiding drag, as far as I am concerned, is effected by casting a curve in your line. You can use either the positive curve or the negative one, depending on the wind direction and the type of fly you have chosen. Both are equally easy to make and the final result on the water is identical with either delivery. The key to curve-casting is to slant your rod to one side of the vertical position and in some situations with the rod work-ing in nearly a horizontal plane.

You make the positive curve cast by adding extra force to the forward motion of the rod or by pulling back on the line with your left hand at the last minute so that your leader and last few feet of your line not only straighten out, but continue on through and curve in the opposite direction. In other words, if the cast is made with your rod slanted to your right, your fly will be traveling to the right of your line before the cast straightens out and then will continue on through and end up falling on the water to the left of your line.

This cast is most useful when there is a slight breeze flowing from your right to your left as this will help the fly travel through and land well downwind of your line. Similarly, if the wind is blowing from left to right, and you're a right-hander, you can accomplish the same thing by bringing your rod over your left shoulder on the back-cast and forcing the fly to travel through to the right side of your line. In either case, the result is a positive curve de-livery.

The negative curve is just as easy. The rod is worked through the same off-vertical plane, but you quit a bit on the forward cast so that the unfurling loop of line never quite straightens out. You can achieve the same result by shooting some extra line at the last moment which steals momentum from the cast. This delivery usually works best when you're working upwind because a headwind will add resistance and insure a pronounced curve. This is definitely the cast to use into a strong wind and the stronger it is, the more nearly horizontal you will want to keep the casting plane of your rod.

Which of the two types of curve casts you should choose will usually be dictated by circumstances and common sense. Wind direction and wind velocity will usually be the overriding considerations. When you're fishing in a dead calm, the type of fly you are using will be the deciding factor. The negative curve is easier to execute with variants, spiders and large flies which offer stiff wind resistance. On the other hand, I find that I can place streamlined flies like standard duns and fluttering caddises more accurately in still air conditions with the positive curve.

With either delivery you can stay in close touch with your fly and impart the slight twitch any time you want after the fly hits the water. Despite the curve in your line and leader even a moderate impulse will be transmitted to the fly because surface tension tends to keep your floating line from moving sideways. This holding action of the water surface is especially noticeable when you make short, sharp motions—the kind best-suited to manipulation of your fly when twitch-fishing.

There are some conditions, like the alder-tunnel I mentioned earlier in the chapter, that seem to defy all the techniques I've described so far and very often these "unfishable" lies are sanctuaries of some of the best fish in the stream. Jim Deren of the Angler's Roost in New York City once pinpointed for me the exact position of a large trout, but added that I'd be wasting my time if I went after him. He described in detail a famous pool on a large river where a good current ran a foot or so out from a cliff on the far side of the river. This fish fed in the narrow band of deep, slack water right up against the cliff and could be seen rising there every evening. The trout, he said, would weigh between four and five pounds—an extremely large brown trout to be a regular surface feeder—but nobody had been able to hook him so far that season.

This particular part of the pool was so deep you had to wade out to your wader-tops to get within casting range. I made a few futile tries for this fish one evening, but quickly crossed off the situation as impossible. Later that year, Jim confided that he had finally hooked that trout and lost it. "On a dry fly?" Jim nodded. "How?"

"I shot a lot of extra line, piling it up in a bird's nest against the cliff. By the time the current had pulled all of it away, the fly had already floated over the fish perfectly and up he came."

That's quite a virtuoso presentation when you're sixty to seventy feet away and up to your armpits in water. Jim certainly deserved that fish. I'm not sure I could bring off a cast like that—even though Jim told me the secret. However, I've thought about that situation a lot since then and I believe I've come up with an easier solution. I'd mark his lie carefully by a bush or tree above him, cross over, poke just the tip of my rod over the cliff and lower the fly to him on the dap. I haven't yet figured out how I'd land him from the top of that twelve-foot cliff, though.

In some situations a fisherman may use several drag-re-

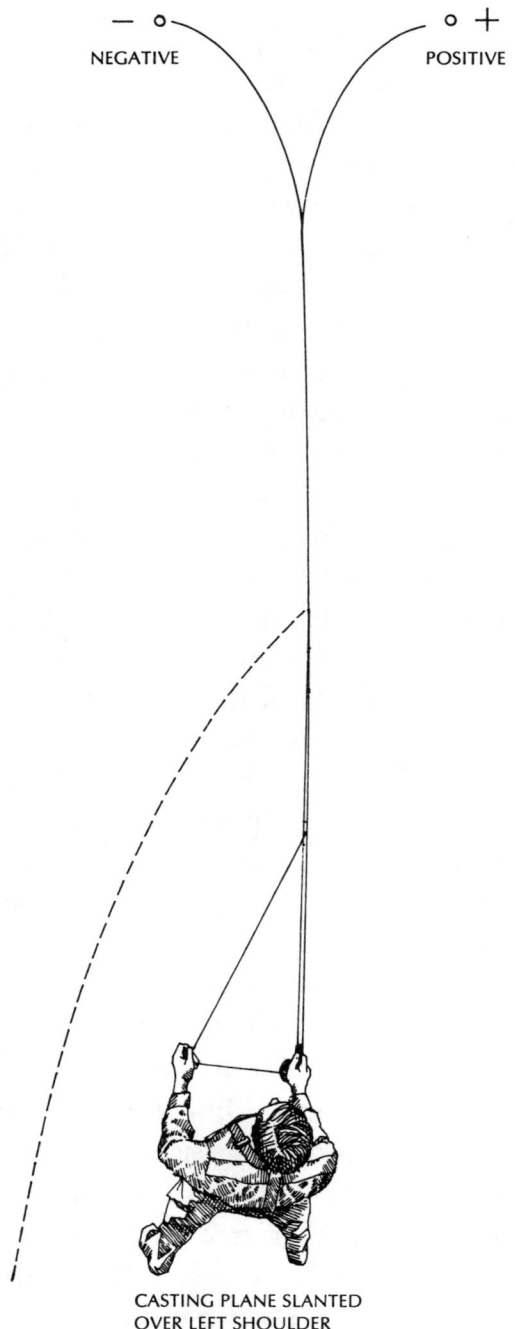

NEGATIVE — ○   ○ + POSITIVE

CASTING PLANE SLANTED
OVER LEFT SHOULDER

Positive and Negative Curve Casts

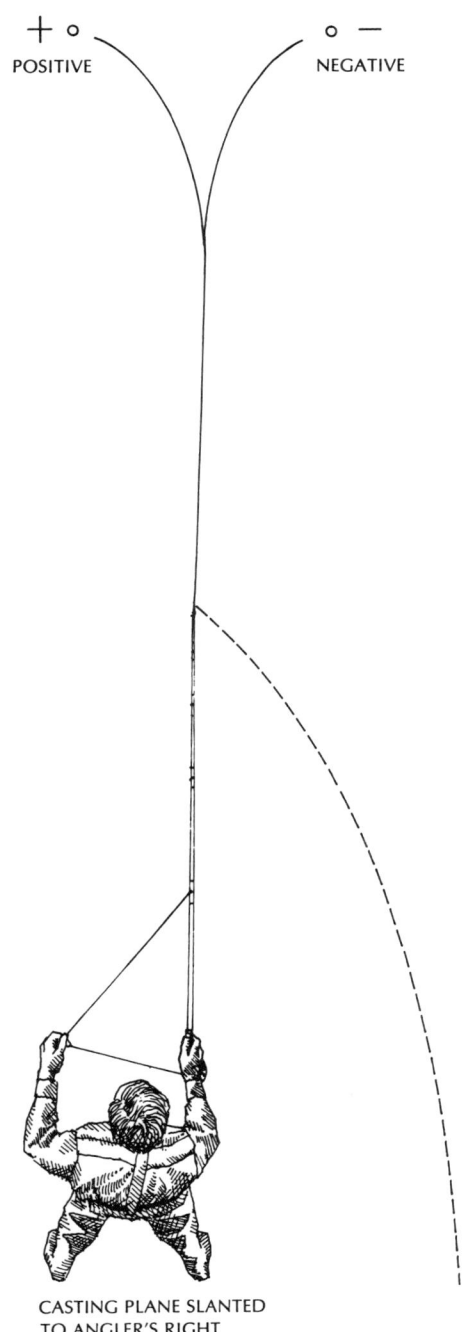

POSITIVE

NEGATIVE

CASTING PLANE SLANTED
TO ANGLER'S RIGHT

Positive and Negative Curve Casts

ducing techniques in a single presentation. He might wade out to a position twenty to twenty-five feet directly oppo-site the lie of a fish—a close approach, but often feasible in streamy or ruffled water—and so keep all but a few feet of his fly line off the water. He could then execute a short curve cast to a spot three or four feet above the fish. Next, as he twitches the fly slightly, he could throw a loop of line upstream to ensure a good, drag-free float over the lie. If no rise occurred, he might decide to fish out the cast into the water below and the best way to produce a long, dead-drift float would be to shake loose line out onto the water in front of him in big lazy S's by wobbling his rod.

This last method of avoiding drag is seldom used in con-ventional dry-fly fishing, but it plays a critical role in the twitch presentation. Especially when you're prospecting and trying to cover as much water as possible with the float that follows the twitch, this method of shaking out loose loops of line is the best way to keep the fly from dragging crosscurrent toward you. If this steady dragging motion is pronounced, there will be little chance of raising a fish during that cast.

If, on the other hand, this cross-stream drag is slight, or if the fly is dragging a bit but only in an upstream direc-tion, the presentation may well be successful. Somehow, trout seem more tolerant of drag when you're fishing with this new method. Perhaps the twitch has aroused their predatory instincts or appetites enough to dull their sense of caution. Perhaps drag in an upstream direction, being more in keeping with adult-insect behavior, is less suspect. Whatever the reason, you can often get away with some drag when using the twitch technique, but don't let this lull you into making sloppy presentations. A drag-free float following the small manipulation of the fly is the most productive practice. Use all your skill and all the drag-reducing techniques to ensure that the fly, once it has started downstream, floats as truly and freely as possible.

10

THE TRACK OF THE TROUT

One of the few advantages the angler has over the trout is that he can stay still and observe while the fish must move as it feeds. This often allows the fisherman to pinpoint the position of a trout before his own presence is detected— an obvious, though valuable head start since trout are widely scattered in even the most productive waters.

The experienced angler, however, can usually learn much more than this from a trout's movements. The fish's relative position in a pool and the type of feeding motion it makes can often help the fisherman—especially one who knows his river intimately—make the right presentation of the right fly to the right place on his very first cast.

I have been able to do this many times on my familiar home water and it's not as miraculous as it sounds. An incident that took place last season will show how rise-forms can often play a key part in helping you select the correct fly and make the appropriate presentation. On this particular June day, high water and cold temperatures had lured me to the river several hours earlier than usual because I expected that cooler water and dim light might set nature's timetable ahead.

My guess was right: fish were already rising in the long pool I had chosen when I reached it at four thirty. A big hatch of size #17 butter-colored duns was in progress and each fly was floating a long way down the pool before it could manage a takeoff in the unseasonable chill. This is a common June-July insect on these waters and I had the appropriate dry artificial already tied on when some inner warning device made me stop and take stock. First, I realized, the trout were taking rather splashily while they usually rise to small, long-floating duns with a dainty sip. Second, the fish were showing at widely irregular intervals and not in the steady pattern that characterizes feeding on a profuse supply of duns. Despite the squadrons of yellow mayflies on the water, the fish were behaving as if they were taking caddis and I decided that they must know something I didn't. I took off the pale dun and tied on a blue caddis—the imitation of a fly I hadn't expected until much later in the evening.

No, I didn't catch the pool Leviathan that afternoon, but I did have excellent sport twitch-fishing with this fly although I saw only a very few caddis on the water or in the air. The pale duns outnumbered them by over 100 to 1 during the entire period, yet the trout seemed to have their hearts set on this larger, darker fly. The two fish I kept for supper were crammed full of the scarce caddis and there wasn't a yellow in either of them. I would have spent a frustrating afternoon if the type of rise-form hadn't supplied a carefully hidden clue.

Trout undoubtedly take their food in any number of ways but, fortunately, most feeding movements fit into distinct patterns which are dictated by the type of food being eaten. For this reason, underwater flashes, shadowy motions and surface disturbances are well worth studying, classifying and remembering. Here, starting on the stream bottom and working up toward the surface, are some of the behavior patterns I have found most common and most revealing.

Perhaps you've noticed the glint of a trout turning on its side right down on the rocks and gravel near the head of a pool or in the slower, deep water just below. I have found this sight especially common at midafternoon during the early part of the season. I have spent many fruitless hours attempting to take these fish. After having tried everything from fast-sinking lines to mended, upstream casts, I now mark down these fish and return later on when they may have given up their bottom-grubbing habits and I'm afraid that's the best tactic I can recommend to you.

There is no proof that the fish I have caught an hour or so later from these locations were the same ones I had seen flashing on the bottom earlier, but the clues I have put together from many such experiences make up a strong case of circumstantial evidence. These fish have been stuffed with caddis-in-case and nearly always with the same species—one housed in a cylindrical case made of fine grains of sand. To this day, I haven't found any effective way to imitate the nearly stationary behavior of these larvae under four or five feet of flowing water. If you feel challenged by this presentation problem, I can only give you my admiration and a word of warning. Big, bronze-sided suckers often give off a similar signal from the bottom, so make sure the fish you've spotted is indeed a trout before you start your labors.

Trout feeding at mid-depth are a far easier proposition.

Here you will seldom be alerted by a glint from the fish's side; more often you will see the fish itself or its shadow because trout do not have to turn on their sides to take drifting food. This is classic nymph fishing and one of the few conditions where I've found the upstream, dead-drift presentation to be superior. Your choice of pattern will have to be based on guesswork or on trial and error since there won't be any ready evidence in insect form to guide you. However, fish feeding in this casual manner are probably taking any likely looking morsel that comes along. I've found that, under these conditions, almost any proven pattern of nymph will work as long as you keep the size relatively small and don't give the fish too much to find fault with.

Many fishing books devote quite a bit of space to tailing trout—meaning trout that are rooting on the bottom in shallow water with their tails waving in the air like bonefish. This may be fairly common behavior on some weed-filled chalk streams in England, but it is extremely rare on other types of rivers. I have seen only one tailing trout in my life and he was as hard to take as the experts had warned. The half hour was well spent, though, for the trout turned out to be a wild brook weighing over a pound—a very good fish for a hard-pounded suburban stream.

When a fish feeding under the surface seems keyed up and nervous in its movements you should be on the alert for a hatch. At first, you'll have to guess at the right nymph imitation from past experience, for trout can become as selective on nymphs as they can on duns when one species is appearing in abundance. Fortunately, this guessing game seldom lasts long because in a matter of minutes some of the nymphs or pupae will reach the surface and give you solid evidence for your choice of imitation. As these flies begin to hatch out, fish will start breaking water as they follow the nymphs to the surface, but if you've hit on the right nymph it is wisest to stick with it until you've seen several winged adults actually taken from the surface.

An across or across and downstream presentation is usually best at this stage of the hatch. If you're not getting many strikes, try manipulating your fly with a few short tugs before giving it up for another pattern. Most fast-water insects are quite active just before hatching, and re-creating the spasmodic movements of a nymph can sometimes cover up for inaccuracies in pattern.

It's usually easy to tell whether trout feeding in this manner are taking mayfly numphs or emerging caddis pupae. Caddis rise from the bottom more rapidly, heading toward the surface at a steeper angle, and trout are forced into making quick, violent darts at these fast-moving targets. Trout often break surface before they can head back down from these feeding passes, and this break makes a distinctive sound. A series of loud "chugs" coming from a run or head of pool almost surely means caddis. Exactly how this noise is made, I have never been able to discover. Rises are irregular and the fish is gone before you can focus on the exact spot. Several English authors have suggested that the sound is made by the fish's open mouth pushing a small geyser of water above the surface. But I lean to the theory that it is caused by the fish's tail churning the water from below the surface because I have been able to duplicate this sound with my hands in a bathtub.

When mayfly nymphs are hatching out in the same sort of water, trout also often break the surface with their tails as they turn back down toward their lies, and I have seen this motion often and clearly. The sound in this case, though, is more of a "splat" and quite distinct from the deep, solid sound I've come to associate with the taking of caddis pupae.

In slow water, nymphing fish seldom break the surface when feeding on either underwater form of insect. Apparently, the whole sequence of action is slowed down so that the trout isn't confronted with a split-second decision. It can see the nymphs or pupae farther ahead and either intercepts them well below the surface or waits to take the emerged fly on the surface when it arrives overhead. When trout in a pool are feeding regularly, near enough to the surface to disturb it and yet are not taking adult flies off the top, they are probably taking small midge pupae.

Once the trout have begun to follow nymphs up to the surface and actually break the skin of the water in their feeding, they will usually take the dry fly as well as the underwater imitation. At this point, I usually switch to the floater—not because it gets more response from the fish, but because it is more fun and, for some reason, I can always hook a higher percentage of the fish with a dry fly.

By the time fish are seen taking adult flies off the top, your choice of artificial is somewhat simplified since you no longer have to consider sunk flies, but you still face the dilemma of choosing the right floater. Some large flies like the March Brown or the Green Drake are nearly unmistakable and selection may be simple. Other flies like the Quill Gordon and the Hendrickson are easily confused, even at close range. It is always wise to capture specimens for close scrutiny, but this is still no substitute for stream observation.

Even the most familiar waters will sometimes serve up a hatch of flies you've never noticed before, and often these float by undetected among the more showy, more familiar specimens. Because of this you should capture specimens, verify which fly is being taken, and note the manner of feeding, as well. The last-mentioned method of gathering information is often the most useful of all, for it can be difficult to collect specimens quickly and you may have to rely on observation alone if you're going to get into action before a hatch peters out. You can gauge the accuracy of your first choice of fly by casting the artificial out next to a natural for comparison. Most of the time this second check, plus a shrewd analysis of the visible rise-forms, is all you need—and indeed all you have—to make a diagnosis.

One of the most important aims of this intelligence gathering is to discover whether the fly being taken is a mayfly, a caddis or some other, less common type of insect. This may not be as simple as it sounds, for there may be several orders and species of insects in the air and on the water at the same time. Yet when insects are plentiful one particular species will be preferred to the exclusion of all others by the better class of trout. For this reason, rise-forms may supply the single most valuable clue.

There's a surprising variety in the ways trout feed on different types of aquatic insects. One of the most distinctive patterns occurs when trout are feeding on caddis—whether in the pupal form or in the adult stage. The main reason for this is that caddis are more evasive targets than mayflies. Most species of caddis get airborne very quickly, even in foul weather, and returning egg layers are equally nimble at getting on and off the water. Trout seem well aware of this and take a quick, violent shot at their quarry, causing a surface eruption very much like the pupal-taking "chug."

Even in slow water, trout seem to take adult caddis with an extra burst of speed—not perhaps with the noisy slash they make in fast water, but certainly with more vigor than when they are sipping mayfly duns. Despite this extra effort, trout miss so many caddies that the sight of a fly zigzagging upwards over a rise-form is one of the surest signs of emerging caddis.

Another sign that should alert you to the possibility of caddis is the frequent splashing of small trout in the slack water and eddies along the shoreline as they leap full-length out of the water to take caddis buzzing overhead. Caddis like to mill around just above the surface in such places and, although large trout seldom make such a grandstand play, the five- to eight-inchers seem to have no qualms about burning up youthful energy this way.

Small trout in the stream margins will also take midges in this leaping manner, but the simplest observations should pin down the insect in question. Caddis are usually comparatively large and exhibit a characteristic, zigzag flight pattern. Midges, on the other hand, are minute and tend to fly in large, undulating clouds.

Trout feeding on either pupal or winged caddis, as I have said, seem to behave more erratically than when feeding on mayfly duns. I don't know whether this is because caddis hatch out less regularly and over a wider portion of the water than mayflies do or whether a trout simply travels farther from its lie to take one of these more active insects and thus pops up in odd places. Whatever the reason, caddis-taking trout are hard to mark down. You may see one come up within easy casting range and then another just beyond and yet, though the pool is wrinkled with feeding fish, these two particular fish may not show again for fifteen minutes or more. Total pool activity may be as intense as when a mayfly hatch of similar size is on, but individual fish are not nearly as regular or as predictable in their feeding. Therefore, the angler must do a certain amount of prospecting if he is to make the most of a caddis hatch, and the method for doing this has been described earlier.

On the other hand, mayfly duns float downstream a lot farther before taking off, and they get channeled into feed-lanes. Trout line up with these food-producing currents and take their choice in a more leisurely, more measured manner. This makes for classic dry-fly fishing conditions wherein you locate a good, steadily rising trout and experiment with imitations until you hit on the right one.

When trout are feeding on duns their behavior can become predictable—even rhythmic. Rise-forms are deliberate, unhurried, and sometimes so delicate that it is impossible to tell whether the fish in question is large or small. The natural fly will disappear from the surface and be replaced by a small dimple with no part of the trout's nose or back breaking the surface.

These are only generalized rules for separating the duns from the caddis. Which type of dun the fish are taking usually will have to be determined by close observation; yet a few mayflies seem to be so distinctive that they induce a special rise-form. The March Browns and their slightly smaller, paler cousins the Grey Foxes are large, succulent flies with pronounced behavioral characteristics which in turn, affect the feeding patterns of trout. These flies have strong, widespread, crablike legs with which they kick and struggle on the surface after hatching. And they seem to have difficulty in getting off the water, even in clement weather. I have seen a March Brown on a sunny, warm day make as many as twelve vigorous attempts to take off before it succeeded in getting airborne. Whether this is caused by high wing loading or by slow development and drying of the wings, I do not know, but it is highly characteristic of these flies and of their relatives in the important *Stenonema* group. As a result, trout become excited and slash at these flies in a manner more characteristic of a caddis-take than of the usual mayfly feeding pattern. Fortunately, these flies are large, highly visible, and their backward-slanting wings make them so easy to identify, even at a considerable distance, that they are one of the easiest hatches of all to diagnose properly.

Another aspect of rise-forms can often help you identify the fly that's emerging—the portion of the pool in which the fish are feeding. The more you know about the insects in your particular river, the more useful this type of information will be. For example, Quill Gordons usually hatch out of fast water or the heads of pools. Hendricksons pop up in slightly slower water or a little farther down the pool. The March Brown and the Dun Variant (*Isonichia bicolor*) tend to emerge in still slower water and often most heavily from the stream margins. All this is useful local knowledge. But remember: a strong wind or exceptionally cool or damp weather can mean that fish will take flies quite a distance from their point of emergence, so use these feeding-position clues with some caution and cross-checking.

Spent mayflies, or spinners, behave quite differently from hatching duns, and trout adjust their feeding habits accordingly. Since these insects are dead or dying, trout feed on them in the easiest possible manner, expending a minimum of effort. Unless there is a large, slow eddy near the head of the pool, spinner-feeding trout will position themselves in the slower, bottom half of the pool or flat, sometimes right down to the lip where the water runs out. The best fish and, in fact, nearly all of the risers, will be in the food-carrying thread of the current, often queued up in line astern formation.

When fish are really on the spinner, they will often leave a dimple so insignificant that you might confuse it with the rise-form of a three-inch dace. At other times, though, the fish will show most of its back above the water in an agonizingly slow motion and then tilt downwards with a satisfied wag of its tail. The few times the light has permitted me to watch this process, I have noticed that the fish lie poised just under the surface and tilt up and down with a rocker motion every time they rise. The whole process looks as if the trout were nearly asleep or in a trance.

If the fall of spinners is profuse, fish will rise in a rhythm so regular that you could set your stopwatch by it. There's no need for them to take every fly and, in this slow water they have chosen, trout set their own hypnotic feeding pace.

Trout will often feed on two other types of insects in almost this same manner. A fall of flying ants will cause similar feeding patterns and so will a gust of jassids or leafhoppers. But both of these usually occur in the early afternoon, during the late heat of the day with ants and while the wind is still strong or puffy in the case of jassids. Flushes of spinners, however, almost always occur just as the light is failing—especially during mid and late summer when this type of food becomes really important to the trout.

Of course, there are almost endless refinements and subvariations to the generalized hatching and feeding patterns I have mentioned. There's one more I'd like to describe because it seems unique in my experience. When fish start rising suddenly during a short squall or rain shower early in the season, I am now almost certain that the fly hatching out is the Quill Gordon. Unlike many other insects, the Quill appears in flushes during spells of bad weather and often shows up under foul weather conditions several weeks after you think the insect is through.

I seem to tuck away one or two new and useful facts on rise-forms and feeding patterns each season. If you observe your favorite river and its familiar flies carefully and objectively, you will undoubtedly do the same or better.

11

KILLING FLIES
AND HOW TO TIE THEM

American dry-fly fishermen, today, are divided into two distinct but friendly schools and the crux of their disagreement is the importance of the pattern of fly. The *Presentationists* believe that knowledge of trout lies, pinpoint casting and an absolutely drag-free float are far more important than the fly they present. They are the direct spiritual descendants of George LaBranche, who founded this school and who stated that a generic mayfly imitation like his famous *Pink Lady* was good enough under most conditions on our rough, infertile streams. More recent Presentationists have claimed that they used exactly the same size and pattern of fly for an entire season and have consistently outfished the compulsive fly-changers. The *Imitationists*, on the other hand, take the Presentationists' skills pretty much for granted and insist that the better trout demand an exact duplication of a particular insect at any given moment and that the ability to match this natural accurately is the key to success.

Each side can muster some pretty telling evidence. The Presentationists' theory usually proves out because most streams today are populated by innocent, freshly stocked trout and because most of our rundown, semipolluted waters seldom serve up a hatch big enough to be worth matching, anyway. The Imitationists are right in their own way: good-sized, wild trout do become preoccupied with an insect of a certain size, shape and color when and if it is hatching out profusely.

The Imitationists seem to be winning out in recent years if literary output is any criterion, but perhaps this is because a new and better artificial gives authors something to write about. The scope for this sort of article or book is almost infinite when you consider the wide range of fly-tying materials, the thousands of insect species, and the many possible styles of tying. A further advantage the Imitationist author enjoys is that artificials and their natural counterparts make striking subjects for beautiful color photographs. Then, too, anglers tend to achieve a certain level of presentational skill and stay on this plateau a long time. They're just human enough to hope that a new miracle fly will help them reap the admiration of their peers in the coming season.

The Presentationists, however, have only a limited bag of tricks and this curtails their printed contributions. Likely trout lies are hard to photograph convincingly and even harder to describe with words. And after you've laid down the fundamentals of curve casting and the wavy S line presentation, you've pretty well run out of stunts.

I'm not going to side with either camp because I'm about to propose a third school of fly fishing: the *Behaviorists*. The main tenet of this just-now-founded school is that your fly will be more effective if it imitates the behavior of insects in general or, when one fly is on the water in quantity, if it duplicates the movements as well as the appearance of that fly in particular.

This new school should gather followers by the hundreds of thousands from believers in the established doctrines, not only because it catches more fish, but because it should convince both the Presentationists and the Imitationists that they have been absolutely right all the time. When there is the usual "nonhatch" this new method can create the illusion of life with a generic imitation indicating that the presentation is the all-important factor. And when there is a glut hatch, close imitation of the size, color, shape and *behavior* of that particular insect will prove to the Imitationists that their theory, too, has always been the correct one.

In the previous chapter I discussed the behavior of various aquatic insects, but I didn't touch on the imitation of the *appearance* of these flies. Here the Behaviorist finds his fly-tying problems doubled, for not only does he have to float a relatively heavy steel hook, but he has to float it buoyantly enough so that he can manipulate his fly on the surface. And yet, this same imitation must duplicate an actual insect as closely as possible.

The question then becomes: how much can you deviate from the natural insect and still convince the trout lying in clear, unruffled water? What does the trout actually *perceive?* This is well-trampled ground and I'm not about to add my footprints to what seems to me to be the turf of the trained natural scientist. Suffice it to say, we Behaviorists are pragmatists and will avoid complicated theories on optic nerves and pupil shapes and put our trust in what has proved to have worked.

We know well enough what an insect looks like to us

when held in the hand and we have studied many photographs showing what the underwater camera records. But how is this same evidence gathered by the trout's eye and evaluated by its primitive brain so that the sight triggers a rise?

There is ample evidence that trout don't perceive the way we or our cameras do. If they did, the presence of the hook alone might be enough to discourage all but the fingerlings from taking. The most sophisticated dry-fly fishers in the world—the British chalk-streamers—learned long ago that trout often fail to respond to the photographically realistic but opaque imitations that Halford designed. For example, the Medium Olive, an olive-dun-colored fly, is most effectively imitated by the Hare's Ear—a brown fly that looks nothing at all to the human eye like the natural. And the Blue Winged Olive, Europe's most important summer evening mayfly, with a very similar color scheme, is generally considered best imitated by the Orange Quill—a fly with a ginger hackle and a bright orange body!

While I have not been able to piece together a logical theory of trout perception based on these and other cases wherein trout vision seems different from ours, I am, nevertheless, convinced that trout see, or see and react, in a way that the camera can't predict. In the first place, they seem unable to count. For example, I have found that a dun tied with ten or twelve whisks for a tail not only floats better than the one with only two or three slips of hackle, but that it fools just as many fish. And even the sparsest of conventional dun dressings presents the illusion of many more legs than the six every insect possesses. Yet even postgraduate, most pounded chalk-stream trout don't find this a deterrent and some of the heaviest-hackled flies in the world are those that have proved themselves for over eighty years against many alternate dressings on these clear Hampshire streams.

Some of the most accurate and lifelike duplications, at least as far as the human eye is concerned, that have ever been offered were the glistening, plastic nymphs that almost every tackle store carried a few years ago. Some of them seemed so lifelike that you expected them to crawl off the hook, and yet they were poor to indifferent producers.

Behaviorists, as I have said, believe in what *works* and I don't think the last word has yet been said on imitations of most of our natural insects. Not only are the species of major aquatics extremely numerous, but there seem to be almost infinite variations of the same species from river to river.

The Quill Gordon, *Iron* (*Epeorus*) *Pleuralis*, makes a good example of how even minor changes in environment can alter the appearance of a fly. Ray Ovington said it is a greyish bodied fly with strong golden bars. Art Flick implies that it has a black-and-white underbelly like the stripped peacock herl used on the body of the artificial. Others have described the body as brownish. But on the river I fish most often, which is within thirty miles of the rivers where Flick and Ovington collected their specimens, Quills have an unbarred, cream-colored underside with just a touch of olive undercolor. I have found that if I tie the body to look like this, it will outfish the standard dressing every single time. (Incidentally, details from Gordon's writings and actual samples of the Gordon-tied fly have convinced me that "The Sage of the Neversink" had quite another fly in mind, but that's a story in itself.)

These endless and sometimes confusing variations in flies

from river to river may be a blessing in disguise, though. They mean there are still infinite possibilities for experimentation and improvement. And this holds out the promise that the angler who does his homework and then ties his own flies will be a jump ahead of the man who buys a pocketful of artificials at the tackle store and proceeds to pound away.

For these and other reasons, I am not going to recommend any specific patterns of killing flies here. Compiling a complete and authoritative list for the entire United States would take several lifetimes of full-time research and such a study would fall outside the aims of this book, anyway. But I do have strong preferences for certain *styles* of tying and *types* of flies that I have found most effective.

I am convinced that a body of herl or dubbed fur is best for imitating mayfly duns. Both materials give a translucent effect that is characteristic of the abdomens of the naturals, especially when viewed into the light as the trout sees them. However, I find most fur-bodied flies too heavily dubbed and I use this material sparingly so that the undercolor of the fly body, represented by the shade of tying silk, shows through when the fly is moistened.

Many authorities feel that wings are excess baggage on duns, and they may be right as far as the trout are concerned, but I have a fondness for them, especially on the smaller sizes of fly. At a distance of thirty to forty feet, especially at twilight, wings are often the only part of the fly you can see. This visibility factor alone is worth the extra effort involved in winging. Classic split wings of starling or some other quill are my usual choice, but only because they show up better than bunched wood duck and other types of fiber wings.

Tails are, for some reason, the least discussed parts of

dry flies and yet they are critical. They have to support the bend of the hook where two-thirds of the weight lies, and if they don't do their job properly the entire fly can be worthless. I usually tie in ten to twelve of the steeliest cock spade barbules I can find because skimping here is self-defeating. In fact, I take a further step to insure good flotation at this end of the fly. I run the tying silk under the bases of the tail fibers after they have been set, which flairs them into a fan shape in a horizontal plane. This not only gives a wider grip on the surface tension, but I like to think it looks more like the splayed setae of the naturals.

Mayfly spinners are the easiest flies of all to tie and materials are also undemanding. Since these insects float flush in the surface film, even mediocre hackle will do. I tie on one hackle only, usually a very pale dun, and clip it top and bottom for the spentwing effect. Much the same result can be achieved by separating the wound-on hackle into two equal, horizontal bunches and fixing them with figure-eight turns of the tying silk. But the first method is far easier and the finished fly is just as good. Bodies should be kept characteristically thin. For this reason I often use fine quill or coarse hair since opacity is no drawback in fading light. Good quality tail fibers are still important, though, because of hook-weight at the tail end. I try to flair the six to eight fibers as widely as possible.

Wet flies and nymphs are, I think, best considered as a group even though some authorities feel that these two types of imitations serve widely different functions. I use both of them nearly interchangeably and, with few exceptions, there seems to be no pronounced trout preference for the one form over the other. It has been my experience that most wet flies are taken for nymphs or emerging duns and not mistaken for drowned, mature insects. It is almost impossible to buy wet flies that serve this function well and most commercial patterns are badly conceived and poorly executed.

To be more truly nymphlike, wet flies should show their wings low over the body and absolutely parallel to it. Wood duck, bronze mallard and similar barred plumages when tied on in this manner make excellent representations of the strongly marked backs of nymphs. They are nearly as accurate imitations of the naturals, when in the water, as are the more conventional nymphal patterns. Perhaps too many nymphs are tied from photographs and preserved samples which give no clue to the appearance of the fluttering, feathery and usually quite large gills along the living nymph's body. The slight motion in plumage wings, as well as in the hackle and in the body materials, may tend to create an overall impression of life far better than the more photographic type of nymph does.

Tying in plumage wings in this manner is, admittedly, very difficult at first. You must place the slips of feathers more on the sides than on the top of the hook and finger them in a special way when securing them with the tying silk. Accurate and detailed description is too complicated to go into here, but any good book on salmon-fly tying will give you the technique. There's a trick to it like wiggling your ears: once you've learned it the stunt seems almost too easy.

In the smallest sizes, these feathers tend to break up, and a reasonable substitute for strip-wings can be created by bunching fibers of the chosen feather along the top of the hook-shank. If you choose this route, however, be sure that the wing-seating area has been built up enough so that the wing *does* lie flat along the body or you might as well pick up some nondescripts from the local hardware store.

The classic, quill-winged wet flies are probably the best imitations of emerging duns. How many of these flies shed their nymphal shucks below the surface has never been pinned down by entomologists for the benefit of fishermen. I believe the answer is very few. In any event, this is usually a transitory, split-second state and one far less likely to imprint selectively feeding trout than either the nymphal or adult stage.

One of the few exceptions to this is the famous Quill Gordon, which does hatch out on the bottom and rise to the surface as a full-fledged adult. Why so many experts tout the Quill Gordon wet fly for these conditions, baffles me. We all know that this fly has dark dun wings and brown leg marking despite the confusion over body color. The yellow-winged, dun-legged wet fly of the same name doesn't even come close. When this fly is expected, I use a modified Greenwell's Glory wet on a #14 hook. I have found no other wet fly or nymph to compare with this more accurate imitation during the early stages of a Quill hatch.

I often tie up flies that are halfway between nymphs and wet flies and I'm not sure this isn't the best way of all. I make the bodies of herl or loosely dubbed fur well picked out, and add two turns of conventional, untrimmed, soft hackle at the head. This fly breathes beautifully in the water. If I were limited to one style of sunk fly only, this is the last one I would give up.

There are two types of dry flies that I have found best for manipulating or twitch-fishing and, since neither is covered in standard fly-tying books, I'll describe the method of dressing these styles for the benefit of fly-tyers. One, the Junior Variant, is quite easy: its herl or dubbed body and flaired, strong tail are tied in the same manner I have recommended for duns, but the hackle is different. I choose two feathers, preferably small spades with a fiber length somewhere between two and two-and-a-half times as long as the gape of the hook. This is almost halfway between the standard hackle length and the size chosen for most variants. In addition, I wind on these hackles dullside forward so that the resulting hackle-buzz is slightly concave when viewed from the front. This not only seems to make the fly skitter better, but helps it to last longer, too, for it delays the crushing of the hackle back along the hook-shank—the inevitable death-process of every dry fly that is not left in trees or fish.

The other and more important fly, the fluttering caddis, calls for a more detailed description. I start out by winding the tying silk back toward the tail, proceeding a little further than is customary, or just a bit around the bend. The reason for this is that most caddis have slightly down-pointing abdomens and because this fly needs more room than usual at the eye-end of the hook. Tie in, at this point, two, at most three, strands of fine herl (pheasant-tail fibers are a good example) and very fine gold wire. Wind the herl up the shank: be careful to keep the body slim and even, to a point just beyond halfway to the eye of the hook and fasten it down. The wire is then wound tightly to the same place with four or five turns, but in an opposing spiral so that it binds the herl down and protects it.

Next comes the wing and this must be put on with great care. I usually make a small bed with the tying silk in the winging area, bringing this up level with the herl so that there will be no bump to the rear that might flair or splay the winging fibers. Take a good spade or shoulder hackle and stroke the fibers backwards until the individual points are evened up and twitch off a section about three-fourths of an inch wide. Position this bunch on top of the hook so that from the tying point to tips it is a bit more than twice as long as the now finished body and bind it down with one full, firm turn of tying silk. If the fibers lie absolutely flat along the shank, you're in business. If not, take them off and build up the wing-bed with thread until it is absolutely even with the hard section of the herl body. When you have wound the body correctly with a suitable, small herl, this is seldom necessary, but these extra turns of silk can remedy any small error.

Once these top fibers are set, place two more bunches of the same bulk and length, one on each side of the hook, and tie them in with one turn each. Now half-hitch or weight the silk and examine the wing from all angles. When viewed from the rear, it should look like the upper half of a small tube, only slightly larger in diameter at the tail end than it is at the tying-in point. It should also veil the body almost completely when viewed from the side. At this point you can still make minor adjustments by pinching and cajoling the fibers where they join the hook. Once you are satisfied with the overall appearance, bind down firmly and finally with three or four turns of silk placed in tight sequence toward the head of the fly.

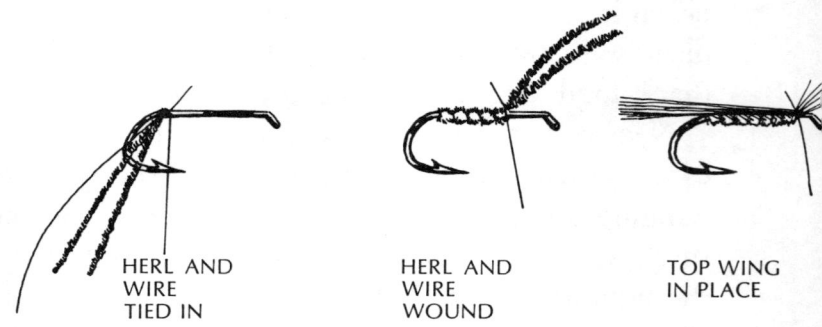

HERL AND
WIRE
TIED IN

HERL AND
WIRE
WOUND

TOP WING
IN PLACE

Tying the fluttering caddis

Take a fine, sharp pair of scissors and trim the wing-butts to form a gradual inclined plane, heaviest near the tying silk and coming to a point just back of the eye of the hook. It's a good idea to hold the wings firmly with your left thumb and forefinger right at the tying-in point while performing this delicate process so that the wing is not jostled out of position at this crucial stage. When the taper is absolutely even, take some transparent head lacquer or DuCo cement and work it into the exposed butts to keep the slick hackle fibers from pulling out during the punishment of fishing. When this cement becomes tacky, tie in two hackles of the usual size for that hook and wind them on in the conventional manner, being careful to bunch them tightly so that they don't slide loosely down the inclined plane toward the eye of the hook. Whip finish, varnish the head, and the fly is finished.

Each caddis represents a larger than average investment in choice materials and in effort, but it's worth it in the long run. If properly tied, it will float higher and take more punishment than any other fly in your box. And, I've found, it will take more fish, too.

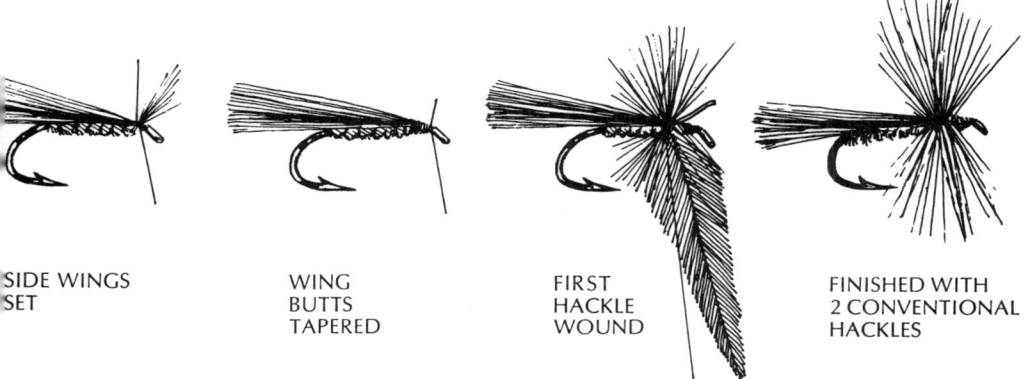

SIDE WINGS
SET

WING
BUTTS
TAPERED

FIRST
HACKLE
WOUND

FINISHED WITH
2 CONVENTIONAL
HACKLES

12

MORE SENSIBLE TACKLE

Fly-fishing tackle has changed more in the past thirty years than it has probably in any entire century. In 1941 most fly rods were made of split cane; today 99 percent that are produced are glass. During this same period, lines have changed from oiled silk to synthetics, and silkworm gut has been replaced by nylon or platyl monofilament. Only reels and hooks remain the same or little changed.

I'm a devout believer in progress, but it seems to me that all these advances have added up to greater convenience rather than better performance. It's like the case of the .22 rifle. It doesn't shoot with any greater accuracy than it did when I was a boy. But with lubricated bullets and noncorrosive primers you don't have to clean it after a day's shooting anymore. Similarly, we no longer have to wipe off and revarnish our rods, dry and grease our lines, or soak our leaders. But can we now present our flies more accurately or more realistically to the fish? I doubt it. In fact, I think we may have taken a slight step backward as far as effective presentation is concerned.

Our new styles in rods are a case in point. Forget materials for the moment and consider their length and strength. Before the war, eight and a half feet was nearly standard, yet today a seven-and-a-half-footer is often called a club and many anglers have chosen rods of six feet or even less. These new, shorter fly rods will drive out a lot of line—more than enough for practical stream fishing —but will they put it out delicately and fish it properly?

Catalogues recommend #6 or #7 weight lines for most of these short rods, preferably weight-forward tapers, and this gives you some idea of their actual strength since this is the weight of line it takes to bring out their optimum action. Such a rod won't pamper a 7x tippet as well as a rod that takes a #4 or #5 line as the latter bends under much less weight. Therefore, a six-and-a-half foot rod that takes a #7 line is not really a light-fishing rod despite its total weight of perhaps only two and a half ounces.

This current light-rod craze is, in some ways, self-defeating. The total weight of the rod tells you little about its casting ability, presentation delicacy or sporting qualities in playing fish. The exact opposite of our theoretical two-and-a-half ounce rod mentioned above is an old Thomas bamboo which I own. It is ten feet long weighs five and a half ounces and takes a #4 line. It is a bit limp for effective dry-fly fishing, either through age (it was built before 1910) or because it was designed as a "wet-fly" action. But it magnifies any fish I hook—even an eight-incher— into a respectable opponent. Elementary physics will explain why this is so.

Obviously, a rod that flexes well with a #4 line will bend under the pull of a small fish more quickly and fully than will a rod that needs a #7 line. But that's only part of the story. The mechanical advantage against your hand

makes a fish seem heavier and scrappier. Since a rod is basi-
cally a lever and the palm of your hand is the fulcrum, a
ten-foot rod gives the fish a more than 50 percent increase
in pull against you compared to the leverage when you're
using a six-and-a-half footer.

The surprising thing is that men who favor short rods
which nevertheless need fairly heavy lines to bring out
their actions tend to quote the lengths and weights of their
rods with a certain smugness. Fish are getting smaller, they
argue, and therefore it's more sporting to use a smaller rod.
Actually, all they are doing is cutting down on some theoretical arm fatigue, but they aren't using an implement that
makes the fish feel stronger. Did you ever wonder why the

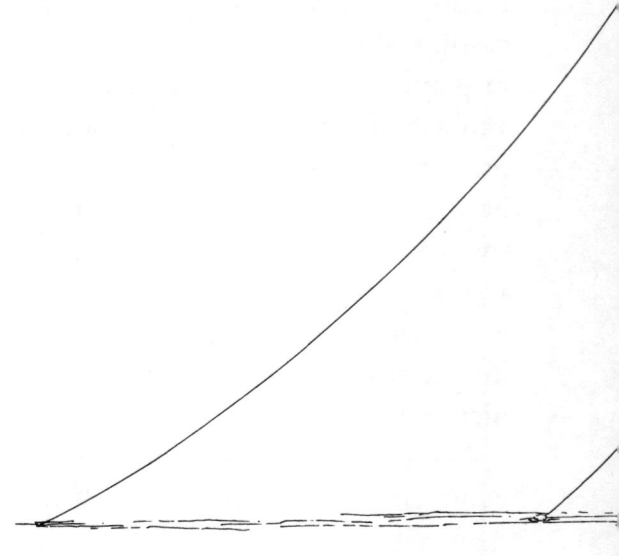

How a long rod with a light line helps

rods used for swordfish and giant tuna are so short? Simply because longer rods, while they might absorb more of the sudden shocks from the fish, would put too much mechanical advantage in favor of the hoped for one thousand-pounder and pull the angler right out of his fighting chair!

The short, stiffish rod so popular today is not necessarily more sporting or more fun than one that is a foot or two longer, no matter what the catalogues imply. On top of this, they are far inferior as fly-presenters on running water because they produce more drag in dry-fly fishing and give you less control of fly-speed when wet-fly fishing. An eight-and-a-half foot rod held at the same angle will keep several more feet of line off the water than a six-and-

prevent drag by keeping more line off the water.

a-half footer will. Since most trout are caught within twenty to thirty feet of the angler, the longer rod may give you a 20 percent advantage in thwarting drag. This is the reason why professional French market fishermen, who, by the way, are the most skillful group of anglers I've ever encountered, use fly rods that are at least ten feet long.

Several years ago, I read an article in a popular sporting magazine extolling the virtues of the six-foot rod for stream fishing. The author claimed that his one-and-a-half ounce stick was not only featherlight and fatigue-free, but that it gave him as good a float and as much line control as the average rod *if he fished with his arm extended vertically over his head.* Fatigue-free? Medieval torturers couldn't devise more excruciating pain than holding that position for a few minutes. Every time I think about it, my heart goes out to the Statue of Liberty. Since reading that article, my trout rods have grown steadily longer. Now I use an eight-and-a-half footer but am looking for a nine-footer that handles as easily.

Some people accuse me of using a "grilse" rod for trout, but that's not the case at all. This rod takes a #5 line and I find I can fish 6x gut (that's gut, not nylon) with it and seldom break off a fish on the strike even when I'm making the long casts necessary for fishing smooth water at dusk. Some authorities would have you believe that a rod of this size would wear down anyone except an NFL defensive lineman, but I weigh only 130 pounds after a big steak dinner and no matter how long I fish, my arm never complains.

The question of bamboo versus glass has been discussed over and over again. Bamboo at its best seems to have a sweeter feel for casting and a greater feeling of intimacy when you're playing a fish. The only explanation I can give for this phenomenon is that bamboo is solid and therefore transmits even the smallest impulses to the hand with greater fidelity. On the other hand, glass is slightly lighter for the same amount of strength, but this is of more importance to the tournament caster than it is to the practical trouter. I think, perhaps, that the greatest benefit of glass is that it will allow us to fish longer rods with less fatigue —if and when somebody decides to design them.

My favorite eight-and-a-half-footer that works with this light #5 line has enough backbone to snap water off the fly when false-casting, and it sets the hook crisply even on long deliveries. The light line itself has two great advantages. It doesn't sag down into the water as near to my rod-tip as a heavier one would—thus reducing the possibility of drag—and it disturbs the water less, both when it lands on the surface and when it is picked off for the backcast.

After trying many types of lines, I have gone back to the old, hard-to-get silk double taper. This is not because of contrariness or nostalgia, but because this line performs better in every way. Silks don't shoot as well as the glassier floaters, but trout fishing is seldom a distance contest. They are denser than the synthetics so they cheat the wind better and they have tips that are 20 to 25 percent finer. This finer point not only disturbs the surface less, but also means you can use shorter, more manageable leaders. When greased properly silks actively repel water and can be picked off the surface for the backcast with less disturbance than a line that floats only because it is a bit lighter than water. Then, too, the tip floats and I have yet to find a floating line on which the last few feet doesn't sink. The extra floatability of greased silk throughout its entire length is an enormous advantage when you're fishing very fine tippets and making long casts—which is often necessary when there's a fall of spinners in the late evening. I have tried to get this same result by greasing my synthetics, but their surface is so mirror-smooth that they don't retain the high-floating coat of grease for more than a few minutes.

The penalty I have to pay for the improved performance of my silk line is, I feel, a small one. When I'm through fishing, I peel off the wet portion of the line into the back seat of my car for the trip home that evening. Dressing the line next day takes only a minute or so and this insures two to three hours of good floating. If I fish longer, I reverse the line on the reel, which also takes about a minute, and have another two hours of fishing with a high riding line. All maintenance takes about two minutes per fishing day and, as this is not during fishing hours, I feel I'm getting a bargain.

The leader situation today is another mixed blessing. Nylon and platyl have two advantages: cheapness and instant use. Strength? The printed figures show that synthetics are twice as strong as silkworm gut, but there's a factor left out of these measurements. The tests are conducted under a slow-load: tension is increased gradually until the strand snaps. This sort of strength is academic, I think, because 99 percent of all trout are broken off on the strike and this is a fast-load situation. Gut can withstand a fast load of short duration with a performance far in excess of its slow-load, or official, rating while the reverse is true of synthetics.

Gut has further benefits. It tends to sink, which makes it much less visible than the floating monofilament tippet. It is also stiffer and presents more predictable and controllable curves and will straighten out more easily on the forward cast without forcing the delivery. It knots more securely and, incidentally, is much less likely to pick up those weakening wind knots that mean the finish of a leader or a tippet.

In fact, I can think of only one big drawback to silkworm gut and that's not the necessary presoaking, but its lack of availability. I still have a two-year supply in most sizes, but I'm desperately short of 4x tippets. I don't know how long the whole stockpile can resist the ravages of age. I will mourn the passing of my small hoard of gut and so will a few friends to whom I have recently given silkworm leaders—fishermen who hadn't used gut for years and had forgotten what a joy it was to fish with.

Hooks are no better than they were before the war, as far as I can see, and the materials we mask them with are getting scarcer by the minute—especially first-rate hackle. Reels haven't improved, either. They're a shade lighter than they used to be, but their clicks sound just that much tinnier and if you drop one it damages easily—often irreparably.

The finest trout reel ever made, in my opinion, was the Hardy Perfect patented in 1890. I have never been able to damage one and they seem to improve with age. I own one that's at least fifty years old and it's slightly smoother running, if anything, than its younger cousins. This reel was discontinued several years ago and replaced by a lightweight series—perhaps to cash in on the theory that a reel that is light on the scales is more sporting because this measurement is applied to rods. One of the few smart things I have ever done was to lay in a last-minute supply of Perfects that will last me my lifetime no matter how cleanly I live.

While I'll stand by every word I've said on tackle so far, I'm probably guilty of perfectionism. There's a lot to be said for the tackle sold today. The modern outfit is much better balanced, on the average, and a good deal cheaper in terms of purchasing-power dollars than those offered several decades back. This alone has done much to popularize fly-fishing, which was once considered the preserve of the expert or the rich. And I'm sure that the sheer convenience of today's tackle is considered a blessing by 99 percent of all fly-fishers and that I'm one of the few cranks who are willing to put up with the extra effort for a relatively small increase in performance.

Equally important, we have a far wider choice today. Despite the popularization of shorter sticks, you can now find rods of more lengths and actions than you formerly could—even at small tackle shops. There's a greater choice of lines and tapers, too, and the new sinking lines have added new dimension to sunk-fly fishing in big waters. Diehards can still get superb splitcane rods if they're willing to pay the price. Silk lines can be obtained from England, where they are enjoying a new wave of popularity. Only silkworm gut seems to have gone beyond our reach.

The trout outfit I now use 99 percent of the time is a compromise: suitable for all types of trout fishing and perfect for some. The rod is an eight-and-a-half foot Hardy Phantom bamboo weighing four and five-eighths ounces. For working pools and flats it's ideal. When I'm fishing a dropper-fly downstream in pocket water, I wish it were a foot longer. And when I'm popping the dry fly upstream into the same sort of water, my wrist tells me it should be shorter. But I can't lug three separate outfits around the river all day.

The line I use with it is a #5 double-taper silk and this, too, is a compromise. It's not quite heavy enough for comfortable fifteen-foot casts nor is it quite light enough to dance a dropper fly most effectively. It does seem tailor-made for 95 percent of the fishing I do, though. While I also carry a #6 line for exceptionally windy weather and a #5 sinker for deep-water nymphing, I find I use these spares infrequently.

This combination is perfect for twitch-fishing in pools and for spent-fly fishing at dusk—the times and places where I catch over 90 percent of my trout. It is excellent for runs, heads of pools and streamy water, and I can make-do with it in pocket-water whether I'm fishing upstream or down. It reduces drag, produces fish, is fun to use, and I can't recommend it or a similar outfit too highly. It's a bit more work to maintain. So was my first .22 with the old ammunition it burned. But I think I learned a lot more about how it worked—and also learned more respect for it—because of the necessary daily ritual. This just might apply to fly-fishing tackle, too.

13

FISH-TAKING TIMES

A friend of mine who usually fishes only once or twice a
year dropped in to see me one Sunday night as I was about
to head back to the city. He came to tell me he was going
to stay up on the river all week long and get in some real
fishing. It was late June, the water was in fine shape, and I
kept envying him all the way home as I fought the traffic
and the heat.

When I checked with him the following Saturday I was
surprised by his report: "I caught only one small trout and
I don't think I saw more than a dozen rises all week long.
Don't tell me this river isn't fished out." I couldn't figure
out what had gone wrong until he added that he'd been
out from daybreak till breakfast every single morning, fishing the dry fly constantly and carefully.

I don't know where the myth that fish bite best at daybreak started, but it just isn't so—not as far as the dry-
fly fisher is concerned and certainly not on cool mountain
rivers. You just might catch an occasional large fish that

has been night-feeding and hasn't yet returned to his lair, but you'll probably have to use bait or a streamer-fly to do it. The water that early in the day is too chilly for the dry fly—insects don't hatch and trout aren't very active.

Temperature readings I took one day at that time of year after a clear, crisp night tell the story. When I got up at six in the morning, the river was fifty-three degrees. By eight it was only fifty-four. At ten, when I started fishing, it had climbed up to fifty-seven. Then things began to happen. Eleven . . . sixty degrees. Noon . . . sixty-three. One . . . sixty-six. Two . . . sixty-eight. Four . . . seventy. Six . . . sixty-nine. Seven . . . sixty-seven. At dusk, which occurred at eight thirty, the temperature was back down to sixty-five.

These figures become significant when you realize that the optimum temperature for brown trout metabolism is about sixty-three degrees. Since a trout's body temperature is regulated by the heat of the surrounding water, this means that when the water is sixty-three degrees the fish should be hungriest and most active. Water temperature is probably the most important single factor in trout fishing. This explains why expert trout anglers are so devoted to the stream thermometer.

There are other factors involved, however, because a lot of trout are taken on the dry fly when the temperature is far from sixty-three degrees. One of these is the availability of food. In late April and early May you can get superb dry-fly fishing when the thermometer reads in the forties, but only, in my experience, if there is a good hatch. Prospecting for trout with the surface fly when there is no visible feeding activity is almost always a waste of time early in the season. In mid-summer, on the other hand, trout may gorge themselves when the water is up to seventy degrees, but only if there is a big fall of spent flies or flying ants.

This is why fly-fishing is so effective. Aquatic insects in general seem to have the same metabolic range that trout do. Early season insects may hatch out at surprisingly low temperatures, but they nearly always emerge during the heat of the day, from one thirty to four, when water temperatures will be highest for that twenty-four hour period or nearest to sixty-three degrees. Evening hatches during the dog days will tend to occur when the temperature is sinking back down toward the optimum sixty-three degree mark. When the thermometer doesn't drop down fast enough after the sun has left the water, most hatches will start after darkness has set in—which explains the effectiveness of night-fishing during extremely hot weather.

This linkage of the hatching-time of insects with the best feeding-temperatures for trout is the rule, but I have seen some notable exceptions. On one mid-May afternoon, I witnessed a heavy hatch of mayflies that lasted a full three hours without seeing a single rise. The water was low and clear, the weather was perfect and I was on one of the most productive stretches of a well-stocked stream. I still can't find a satisfactory explanation for the trouts' lack of appetite—unless they had gorged on nymphs during the morning before I reached the river and were recovering from indigestion. In any event, such occasions are rare indeed: you can almost always count on feeding fish when flies are plentiful.

Light, or the lack of it, also plays an important role in the feeding habits of trout. In early spring, when trout are recovering from their winter starvation, fish may feed heavily under the bright noonday sun. This happens to be the period when most food is available and perhaps trout feel less vulnerable in the deeper water and faster, more ruffled currents of spring. But once the long summer sets in and low-water conditions are the rule, pool-dwelling trout stay hidden most of the day till the sun leaves the water. Fish may still feed occasionally in the runs, riffles and pockets when the sun is bright, but most of the stream population will wait for the concealing shadows of evening to fall across the water before they will risk feeding at the surface.

There's one exception to the general rule concerning early spring fishing that I can't explain: unseasonable heat at this time of year seems to put both the flies and the fish off—even though this means that water temperatures will be much closer to the optimum sixty-three degrees than usual. My records show that those prayed-for days in April and early May when the air temperature soars up into the high seventies or low eighties and when you can almost hear the leaf buds unfolding are uniformly disappointing. Apparently stream temperatures of five to ten degrees above normal inhibit early-season hatches and, with this important stimulus lacking, trout are surprisingly dour despite the increased activity of birds and the bursting of buds.

Barometric readings are another important indicator of fish-feeding activity, but I think there's a hidden factor involved here that's more important than the effect of pressure on the fish's lateral line. After all, a 4 percent change in atmospheric pressure is the difference between bluebird weather and the eye of a hurricane. A fish's lateral line undergoes this much pressure change in a split second when he rises or sinks a mere eighteen inches in the water. I think there's a better explanation of why a high barometer means good stream fishing. This takes us back to temperature again.

During overcast, low-barometer periods in summer, river temperatures will hover around the perfect sixty-three degree mark nearly all day long and yet most anglers find this makes for indifferent fishing. On the other hand, bright, crisp, high-barometer days are almost always the best. The reason for this is, I think, that stream temperatures fluctuate more widely during this latter sort of weather and that it is actually *the rate of change toward the optimum* that stimulates the fish into heavy feeding rather than the high-metabolism temperature itself.

I have come to this conclusion because lakes and large salmon rivers, which don't heat up and cool off so dramatically each day, often fish very well in the cloudy weather which usually accompanies a sluggish barometer. Streams and small rivers, on the other hand, having a high proportion of their total water exposed to the air and to the sun can experience a daily temperature fluctuation of as much as fifteen or twenty degrees when clear skies bring cool nights followed by hot, sunny days. On these smaller waters, I find barometric pressure changes have the most marked effect.

Let's return now to the day that I mentioned earlier in this chapter when I recorded water temperatures at regular intervals. I find that I can predict fishing patterns during that sort of weather and at that time of year with surprising accuracy. The morning fishing will begin to get productive about eleven when the temperature is rising rapidly and approaching the sixty-degree mark. The fishing will then be uniformly good until about one, when the thermometer climbs over sixty-six degrees. Admittedly, the temperature is bracketing the optimum figure during that period, but something else is going on. The *rate of change of temperature* is also greatest during that period and on such days I can count on good dry-fly fishing within those hours even when no insects are hatching. The rapid change in temperature around the ideal figure seems to give the fish an added impetus to take up feeding stations and even though there is no visible surface action, trout will often savage the fly the first time it passes near them.

The evening fishing, under these same weather and water conditions, will almost certainly be best from seven until dark. Here, three factors will be operating together. Fading light will induce trout to leave their hiding places and take up more exposed feeding stations. A hatch of flies or a fall of spinners, or both, will supply the stimulus to make trout feed on the surface. But, perhaps most important of all, the water temperature will be dropping sharply toward the trout's preferred range. This seems to be the most important element of all, for the last hour of fishing on summer evenings is likely to be good, whether or not the insects appear in large numbers.

During heavily clouded weather, on the other hand, when the barometer is low and the river never cools below sixty at night nor rises above sixty-five during the day, the fishing is seldom up to what your stream thermometer tells you it should be. Action is slow all day long: trout may rise occasionally, but without regularity. They take grudgingly and, unless there is a freshening rise in river-level, life seems to be proceeding at one-quarter speed during the entire period. The only explanation I have for this state of affairs is that the fish, operating at high metabolic efficiency during the entire twenty-four-hour period, are continuously well fed and are not eager to make mistakes at any particular time of the day. Insect hatches follow the same pattern during this sort of weather. Insect-trout metabolism seems to be synchronized: flies will hatch out in ones and twos over a long period and never seem to stampede the fish into a flurry of surface feeding.

A sudden rise in water changes all the rules. This transfusion of water into the river seems to affect both insects and trout regardless of temperature or barometer. It often stirs insects to hatch out in significant numbers, and even when this doesn't occur, trout will start to take the fly willingly. Of course, I am referring here to modest rises of a few inches. A true spate that muddies the river can have a dampening effect on dry-fly fishing even though the sunk-fly man or the bait-fisher may make a killing.

In July or August, after days of uniformly low water, a river rise of just a few inches following a thunder-shower seems to stir up all the residents of a trout stream as surely as a full spate affects stale salmon that have been imprisoned in a low-water pool. Often there will be an unexpectedly good show of insects triggered by the quickening flow. I have seen exciting hatches of late evening duns and caddis under the glaring midafternoon sun at times like this. Even if insects fail to appear, trout will quickly man their feeding stations and take any reasonable, properly presented fly with an eagerness you haven't seen since mid-May. The sight of water bulging up over the sun-baked stones of the stream-margin is one of the surest signs of excellent midsummer fishing.

One seldom-mentioned factor that seems to have a strong effect on our dry-fly chances is the wind. It is certainly unpleasant to slam a fly out into the teeth of a gale all day long or to have the wind beat down your backcast if it comes from the opposite direction, and yet there seems to be more to it than that. I thought for years that the wind chopping up the surface made rises seem less common only because they were less visible. I also supposed that strong winds blew flies off the water faster and thus gave less stimulus to the fish. I have recently come to a different and more discouraging theory: flies, except perhaps for the earliest and hardiest species, seem to hatch out less frequently when a stiff breeze is blowing. How aquatic larvae in the security of the depths know what is going on above them, I cannot imagine, but it appears that some wind-warning device is one of their instincts and perhaps a necessary one for their survival. Strong gusts could blow the weak flyers out of range of the river and prevent their return for egg-laying.

Whatever the mechanism, I am now convinced that most aquatic insects suspend hatching operations during periods of violent wind. I have marked down good fish that were rising fairly regularly during squally weather. When the wind picked up for ten or fifteen minutes, no more rises would occur. I am quite sure of this for I was observing the ruffled surface carefully at close range. Then, during a lull, the same fish would start rising again as if nothing had happened. A spell of sharp wind seems to keep both the flies and the trout down and is bad news for the dry-fly angler.

During periods of very high barometric pressure there will be an unpleasant bite to the air in the evening which will make you wish you had brought along a good sweater. Almost invariably, this chill will stop the trout from rising although the conditions seem perfect in every other respect. The great deterrent here is that the air has become colder than the water and under these conditions all salmonids refuse to poke their noses out of the warmer water.

This reluctance to rise into the colder air is axiomatic with Atlantic salmon. Not only will they refuse to take the dry fly under such conditions, but they will usually let a wet fly pass by, too, unless it is fished well down in the water with a sinking line. Their cousins the trouts are equally shy about exposing their sensitive noses to a chilly atmosphere. Whenever the air is colder than the water, you can cross off dry-fly fishing as a waste of time.

They say that when there is mist on the water in the morning or in the evening, fishing for both salmon and trout will be poor. In my experience, this is quite correct. When there is little or no wind to circulate the air, this mist forms where the much colder air has prolonged contact with the warmer water.

High humidity, especially when the air feels heavy and oppressive, is perhaps the worst condition of all. Even sunk-fly fishing falls off in muggy weather. However, if rain is falling or starts to fall, the fishing can be quite good, and you may even do well with the surface fly if you can manage to keep it afloat.

The fluttering caddis-fly imitation that I use so often is an outstanding performer under these conditions. Since it is the best-floating fly I have ever seen, it rides cockily on the surface through drizzle and even steady rain. Large, pelting raindrops can sink it, of course, but I think they also drown any natural flies on the water. So true top-water fishing is of little use at such times, anyway.

I can't explain how rainfall can relieve the dampening effects of high humidity, but I do have two hypotheses. One is that the rain knocks flies off streamside trees and bushes into the water and creates a soggy sort of hatch. The other is that raindrops pelting the river-surface add oxygen to the water and that this stimulates the trout. In any event, rainfall—short of a violent thunderstorm—can mean good catches to the summer angler.

On some summer evenings—although on not as many as our memory would have us believe—the wind drops when the hills block the sun from the river. The heat of the day disappears. The air is neither cold nor warm, but has the ideal softness of a spring day. You can *feel* that the fish are going to start rising and under these conditions I've found that they always will.

There's an old saying that the best time to go fishing is when you can—and I've never heard anyone argue with that. The only really bad fishing is no fishing at all. No day during the open season is hopeless. And, if you observe and experiment, it's surprising how much you can enjoy and learn on days when the fishing is, indeed, absolutely rotten.

14

FISH-TAKING PLACES

For many years my knowledge of trout lies was gathered by two simple methods. In some cases I actually saw a fish as it scurried away for cover ahead of me. At other times I located their positions from the rise-forms they made on the surface. The latter observations were usually the most useful, but I have since discovered that these sightings can be misleading.

Fish actively feeding will often be drawn a long way from their holding positions by an abundance of a certain type of food in a particular area. This is especially true of trout which inhabit pools. For instance, fish feeding on emerging duns at the head of a pool in the early afternoon may well be the same ones you saw the evening before at the very tail of the pool while they were sipping spinners one hundred or two hundred yards downstream.

I discovered this the hard way many years ago after I had raised and pricked a large trout at the tail of a long pool just as darkness fell. I went back for that particular prize mornings and evenings for several days and yet I never saw the fish in that location again. What I didn't realize till then was that this fish had his resting lie farther up the pool and had drifted downstream on that particular evening under an especially generous supply of spent flies.

Since then I have added two more methods to my trout-locating repertory. This new research has changed a lot of my previous ideas about where the majority of the trout spend most of their time. I have discovered that the places where they are caught—riffles, runs, pockets and heads of pools—are not necessarily the areas of densest trout population. They are merely the places where the ruffled water surface makes it easier for fly-fishermen to fool any fish which happen to be there.

Of course, any discussion of trout lies should be prefaced by a description of the habits of the various species of trout. Rainbow trout are far fonder of fast water than are brooks and browns. They prefer deep, rapid runs and are sometimes caught in rushing white water where a brown-trout fisherman would never bother to make a cast. Most brook trout, on the other hand, will choose lies in the slower, more exposed parts of the stream. Perhaps this is due to the fact that larger, more aggressive brown trout often chase them out of the choicest lies. I know of one river which contains all three species and the way they sort themselves out into different water types provides a vivid example of their different water preferences. Brown trout seem to choose water that is slower than the rainbow's favorite lies, but faster than the currents usually selected by brook trout. Most of the observations in this chapter deal with waters containing either brown trout exclusively or a mixture of brown and brook trout.

A few years ago when I began feeding the wild trout in

a small river a supplementary diet of floating lights, some of my previous ideas about trout positions were skaken. I soon noticed that fish rose to this ground meat in good numbers all the way down the pool and that there seemed to be no concentration of trout at the head where the current poured in—even though this was the place where most of the fish were being caught. As this distribution of trout seemed to be the rule in nearly all the pools and long flats where I fed, I decided to check and make sure that the fish were truly residents of the parts of the pool where they appeared and were not merely following the food down from the riffle at the head.

I chose a sunny, windless midmorning when visibility would be at its best for my next experiment. I crept up a steep bank overlooking a good pool and started observing the water below. I was positioned about two-thirds of the way down the pool where the current flowed slowly at a depth of three to four feet. With the sun high and slightly behind me, I didn't even need polaroid glasses to make out the small pebbles and caddis cases lying on the bottom.

I soon picked out several suckers and then I saw a small trout, much better camouflaged, hovering in mid-current. For fifteen minutes I observed, taking an informal trout census of the area under clear view, a patch of about fifty feet by thirty. I counted six trout in all, four in the five- to six-inch range and two in the eight- to nine-inch category as well as four much larger chubs. Frankly, I was disappointed with this meager inventory, but the game wasn't over yet.

A shout to my accomplice 150 yards upriver was the prearranged signal for him to start tossing handfuls of ground lights into the riffle above, spreading the food generously across the width of the stream. I soon heard the plops of feeding trout upriver, but it seemed nearly two minutes before the first red specks of lights floated into view.

I had no idea, before this, what two pounds of lights looked like as it floated down a pool. It may not seem like much in bulk or weight when you carry it to the river, but once it churns through a rapids and separates into individual particles it seems literally to blanket the water. I peered intently at my chosen patch of river as the red tide of this instant hatch began to cover the surface below me. A small trout blipped to the surface and streaked down warily toward the bottom. Then, another made a darting rise and, in a matter of a few seconds, all the trout and the chubs I had marked down before were rising confidently and regularly.

Suddenly I noticed a much better trout, a twelve-incher, feeding with the others. Where had he come from? If he'd drifted downstream with the artificial hatch, I'm sure I would have seen him earlier. I looked up-current for approaching fish, but saw none. Then, when I turned my attention back to my chosen sector of water, there were four good fish feeding—no, there were five and all ran between eleven and fourteen inches.

And this is the way a good hatch works. A trout river seems to operate on the same principle as a henyard: once a few fish start feeding the others join in, even though they may be crammed full of food. With trout, though, the smaller fish always start feeding first, and the larger are only pulled to the surface after the hatch and the rising has proceeded for a considerable length of time. Perhaps this is why truly large trout rise toward the end of a two- or three-hour hatch while a half-hour flurry, no matter how intense, seldom affects the sixteen-inch-and-over class of trout.

The trail of lights was thinning out now so I decided to concentrate on one sizable trout and follow his course back to his mysterious lie. This fish soon stopped surface feeding since the trail of lights had now passed on down-current, yet he hovered at mid-depth with his fins quivering— obviously on the look-out for another gift of manna from above. I kept my full attention on this one fish for five or ten minutes and then curiosity got the better of me. I stole a quick glance downstream to see if the other trout I'd ob- served were still in their feeding stations and, when I turned back to my original subject, he had disappeared.

I have since repeated this experiment several times in an attempt to find out where these trout come from and dis- appear to, but in every case the trout have just faded away or my attention span has been broken before I could track a good trout back to his holding lie. There was no indica- tion, though, that the trout had moved off to another part of the pool. They seemed to melt into the stream bottom, and I suspected that they slid under flat rocks or edged up under the undercut sides of boulders.

The only way to check out this hypothesis was to ex- plore the river with mask and snorkel. This is chilly work because the river in question rarely gets to a comfortable seventy degrees. But I chose a hot afternoon and launched myself at the head of this long pool and started to coast quietly downstream with the gentle current. For the first time, I was getting a true picture of the trout's world. The rocks and depressions in the river bottom stood out clearly as hiding or resting places. The under-surface of the wa- ter's skin was a silvery sheet that undulated gently and seemed to press down heavily on the main body of water. The whole effect was that water is more like gelatin than a liquid.

Another surprising thing was the way trout accepted my presence in their element. I could drift within four or five feet of them in most cases before they veered to one side of me, showing more suspicion than alarm. Perhaps they mistook me for a log drifting down-current. In any event, I was no longer the object of terror I was when I appeared upright, wading near the shore.

I began to search for possible hiding spots, submerging for a closer look when I found large flat rocks or interesting undercuts. Once in awhile this close approach would send a good trout scurrying, but I didn't find nearly enough of them to explain the total population I had estimated from my lights-feeding experiments. Since that day, I have repeated this bone-chilling exploration many times with the same results: I can't find more than a quarter of the fish I know to be in the pool no matter how carefully I poke and peer into nooks and crannies. And yet, I think the census I take when feeding lights gives the accurate picture of the pool population and its distribution. Perhaps, when I buy a wet-suit and explore during less comfortable times of day, I'll solve this mystery.

One thing I have learned from my underwater fish counting is that the larger trout do not always inhabit the deepest water. I have explored many pools that are eight to ten feet deep only to discover that the biggest trout in the pool—a solitary old cannibal—has his hiding place in a scant two or three feet of water. A large trout appears in the same lie, year after year near the shallow tail end of a very deep pool. He lies under a great slab of rock not two feet below the surface and fades slowly back into his cavernous retreat whenever I approach. Apparently, it is the degree of protection and possibilities of even further retreat that attract the larger fish rather than depth of water. Unfortunately, such specimen fish seldom engage the dry-fly angler—unless he's willing to go out at midnight.

Trout seem to have a strong preference for certain types of bottom cover against which they appear to be more difficult to detect. They won't lie over a sandy bottom if there is rock, coarse gravel or rubble nearby. Similarly, they avoid lying over a continuous sheet of ledge rock. I know several places where current concentration and depth are ideal for brown trout and yet I never take a fish there because the bottom, at that point, is smooth rock. Trout seem to feel vulnerable over a monotone background and will avoid holding there if any other alternative presents itself.

Patches of freshly disturbed rock or gravel are seldom attractive to trout, but for quite another reason. Until rocks grow a soothing layer of algae, they probably feel like sandpaper to the soft underbelly of the fish. This fact may save billions of trout eggs from destruction every year. I have noticed that when trout are spawning during a spell of exceptionally high water they will always make their redds over the slippery stones that have been covered even during low water. They are not tempted to dig out the abrasive stones in the stream-margin where their eggs would soon be left high and dry.

My experiments with lights and snorkeling have yielded two bits of information that have helped me locate good trout lies even on strange water. The first is that trout choose their holding spots according to a strict set of priorities. First of all comes safety. Trout will put up with a lot of inconvenience to possess an attack-proof sanctuary, and the most secure lies will usually hide the best fish. Comfort is the next consideration. Trout won't take up residence where the current is exhaustingly strong or where the bottom is not to their liking. Last of all comes the availability of food. Fish are willing to travel quite a distance to the food-bearing current as long as they are secure and comfortable during their resting hours.

The other thing I have learned is that pools and especially long, deep flats hold far more trout than fishing results would indicate. This knowledge has helped me greatly on heavily fished streams and, as we shall see in the next chapter, it has allowed me to enjoy more productive fishing hours per day—or per season—than ever before.

15

STRETCHING YOUR FISHING

For the great majority of trout anglers, a day's fishing means a few hours on the river sandwiched between two long and exhausting drives. Most good trout fishing is now so far removed from the centers of population that even a weekend outing may leave you feeling that you've done more driving than fishing. Because hours spent on a favorite river have become so few and so precious, it's a good idea to plan your day so that every minute counts.

In spring, the fishing usually comes to a peak shortly after noon and this is ideal for the day fisherman. But once June has arrived, fish-feeding times occur during less convenient hours and you have to use ingenuity to make the most out of what your travel schedule allows you. Whether you fish at a furious pace or adopt a more leisurely attitude, you'll make contact with more fish and better fish if you suit your fly-fishing method and your position on the stream to the fishes' habits at each given period of the day. Since I have no idea of when your timetable will allow you to reach the river, I'm going to start our hypothetical day at daybreak and fish till dusk—even though few of us are physically or psychologically able to put in a sixteen-hour fishing day.

Dawn offers you one of the best chances to catch the trout of your life. You won't do this every day—in fact, you won't do it very often—but large cannibal trout may still be cruising around at this time trying to catch a last minnow or crawfish before holing up till the next night. Choose a part of the river where there are rock caverns, undercut banks or big snags in deep water, but don't feel you have to concentrate your efforts at the exact site of the suspected lie. Large trout often forage in the shallows or at the heads and tails of pools, and you should prospect throughout the vicinity. A minnow-imitating streamer fly, fished across and downstream, will probably be your best bet. Don't expect a lot of action: this is big game hunting and one hit can make the whole day unforgettable.

By eight o'clock you'll probably tire of this all-or-nothing-at-all game, and it's time to switch methods, anyway. Change to a large wet fly or nymph—one imitating a large stone fly is a good choice—and start working the deep runs and heads of pools. You won't take such heroic fish here, but you're likely to get some distinctly good ones—up to two pounds should be well within your expectations if the river is a good one.

By ten to ten thirty the water will have warmed up a bit and you'll probably start noticing a few insects and some rising trout. This is the second best time of day for the dry-fly man and you should change to a lighter leader and the floating fly. Runs and heads of pools are productive spots at this time, but river traffic is picking up now, too,

and you may find choice spots occupied by other fishermen. Rather than playing an abrasive (and usually unre-
warding) game of musical chairs with your fellow anglers,
it's wiser to head for the flats and pools. You'll find little
competition here and, as we saw in the last chapter, there
are lots of good trout. Best of all, they probably haven't
been hectored by other fishermen since the evening before
and chances are they're relatively calm and receptive.

Here, as I've pointed out before, twitch-fishing with a
floating caddis or a small variant can be highly productive.
Some mornings you will see quite a few rises and this will
help you locate fish, but even if you see no surface feeding,
prospect down the pool. Fish should be at their feeding
stations from now until after noon. I have enjoyed some of
my most exciting morning-fishing on days when I saw
only one or two trout rise to naturals.

If you are fortunate enough to be on private or un-
crowded water, by all means fish the whole river. I often
twitch-fish a long flat and, when I come to the rapids
below, change to a leader with two wet flies on it and
dance the dropper down through the pockets and riffles.
You can miss a lot of enjoyment if you stick to one fishing
method or one type of water all day long.

By one, or soon thereafter, the action will begin to taper
off. This is the time to open your package of sandwiches
or head for the nearest diner. The next few hours will
usually be the least productive of the day, but you can put
them to good use.

When the sun is at its peak, visibility is at its best, too.
Put on your polaroids and inspect some of the pools or
runs you fished earlier in the day. You'll undoubtedly discover many small pockets, undercut rocks and other fish-
holding spots that escaped your notice in the morning.

Tuck this information away for later in the day or for your next trip.

From two till four you can usually take a fish or so if you feel you must keep at it. Look for branches and bushes that hang over deep water and cast your dry fly into the shade below them. Approach these places cautiously and let a small dry fly float through dead-drift. If this fails to produce, put on a caddis and try the twitch. Trout, even in a cooling shade, can be logy at this time of day and it may take a struggling fly to get them up.

When the wind is strong or gusty in the early afternoon, you have a chance to try out a method that I've found exciting. I always carry a small spool of light monofilament in my vest and I make a thirty to forty foot leader out of this gossamer material. To the end of this I attach a bushy variant and work the large, ruffled pools or flats downwind, using the British blow-line technique. This is half kite-flying and half fly-fishing. As you raise or lower your rod tip and as the wind picks up or drops off, your fly will bounce, skitter, hover and dance on the water. Pick a good-looking lie or a known fish-holding spot and work it over thoroughly. If you are persistent enough, you can bounce some surprisingly good fish under the midday sun with this tantalizing technique. A dead-drift presentation would go unnoticed at this time of day, but this dancing presentation will goad trout into rising—another good example of the effectiveness of the moving dry fly.

By four you're getting back into prime fishing time again—if you pick the right stretch of river. Requirements for good, early afternoon water are rigid, but you can find a few of these sections on most streams. Look for a North-South running stretch that has a pronounced hill lying just to the West of it. Ideal locations are in full shade by two thirty to three and fish will have had plenty of time to move into their feeding stations before you get there. Trout will start rising and insects will begin to hatch out here two or three hours earlier than they will on portions of stream that get the full glare of the afternoon sun.

You have a choice of three fishing styles in this situation and each of them should be effective here. You can try the pockets and runs with a downstream dropper, fish this same water upstream with the conventional, dead-drift dry fly or twitch-fish the caddis down through the pools or flats. This latter method is usually my choice at this time of day because it is both more leisurely and more productive. It provides me with a few good fish before the late evening flurry begins and I find this a great psychological advantage. If I've already enjoyed some good fishing, I can approach the evening rise without that feeling of last-chance desperation which is so often self-defeating.

When seven arrives, you should get set for your last stand of the day. It's usually best to move out of your shade-protected section to a piece of river which has, until recently, been under the afternoon sun. Nature's timetable will be set back an hour or two here and you may catch the beginnings of the same hatches or falls of spinners you've just enjoyed at your midafternoon location.

A pool will be your best choice in late evening: it will fish well now and it will soon be hard to follow your fly in fast water, anyway. Start at the head where the current flows in and, if the fish are already rising to duns, put on a good imitation of that particular species and fish it up and across-stream in the orthodox manner. If, on the other hand, you see few rises, you will do well to prospect this water with a fluttering caddis or with a variant fished in the same manner.

In either event, look down the pool at frequent intervals to see whether or not the fish have begun to rise in the slow water. When you see quite a few rise-rings appearing right down into the tail end of the pool, you can be fairly certain that a fall of spent flies has started and you should walk down the shore for closer observation. There are now probably only forty-five minutes left until dark and you must use every moment of this shrewdly. This can be either the most rewarding or the most frustrating fishing of the day, depending on how you approach it.

It's usually wise to spend the first ten minutes of this period without making a single cast. Tie on the size and pattern of spinner imitation you have found most successful on recent evenings or at that time of year and watch the water closely. Pick out several fish that are rising at short, regular intervals and try to estimate their sizes. If they're showing their backs when they come up, this will be easy. If, on the other hand, they're just making surface dimples, as they more often do, you will have to base your size estimates on the locations they have taken up. Usually, larger trout will commandeer the choicest spots—where a slow current-tongue flows close to a deep, undercut bank, for example. This is not an easy game, and never a sure one, but you'll find your guesses will improve with experience. In any event, these hunches will usually be all you have to go on for, even with polaroids, you will rarely see the fish itself in this dim light.

When you have decided on two likely fish, preferably a good distance apart, wade out cautiously to a position directly across-stream from the lower fish. Do not attempt a cast till all your ripples have died down and the fish is rising rhythmically again. Now make your presentation with an upstream curve in your line to keep the leader away from the trout and watch the water intently. If the dimple appears again, pull gently on your line, but do not strike. In case the fish has merely taken a nearby natural, the wake created by your strike will put the fish down for good. You usually can't see your flush-floating fly on the water, but if he has it you'll know soon enough. A steady tightening on your line is all that is needed to set the hook.

If this fish continues to rise, but ignores your fly even though you've covered him a dozen times or more, you still have time to change your fly. More often than not, a smaller spent-wing pattern will turn the trick, for good trout will feed on the spinners of the duns that were too small to attract them earlier in the day.

If you take this fish—but only then—move on upstream quietly and have a try at the other fish you marked. It pays to concentrate on one fish at this time of day. If the spent flies he's taking are quite different from the fly you're using, chances are he won't take it, but neither will the other fish so stick to the same riser till you hit on the right size and pattern. Any summer evening when I take one good trout during this last half hour is a success. Two fish is a bonanza. I can count on the fingers of one hand those occasions when I have landed three.

This, as far as I'm concerned, is the end of our hypothetical, sixteen-hour fishing day. I'll leave the night-fishing to others. A half, or even a third, of this sixteen-hour period should be enough to satisfy, or exhaust, the average angler. Unless I'm experimenting with new techniques at odd times of day, I'm usually satisfied with the best four dry-fly hours: from eleven to one and from seven till nine.

Not only do fishing days seem too short, but seasons come to an end all too soon, as well. Many trout fishermen head for lakes and salt water when summer arrives. While

I'm pleased with the lighter traffic on our streams, I can't help feeling that these deserters are missing some of the most interesting fishing of the year. The state in which I live gives us a six-month open season and I try to make the most of it.

Midsummer and September fishing can be excellent. Even though hatches are often sparse or nonexistent, it's a rare evening when you won't see at least a few caddis flies buzzing over the surface. Since I've started using the twitched-caddis technique, my late season fishing has become more than twice as productive as it used to be, and other fishermen whom I've converted report similar results.

16

HEADS AND TAILS

Over the years, I have picked up odds and ends of useful information on fishing and tackle which didn't fit into any of the preceding chapters so I'm giving them a short chapter of their own. Not all of these are my own discoveries but, since I can't remember ever seeing any of them in print before, I'm passing them on in the hope that you'll find them valuable.

Debarb your trout-fly hooks—especially the dry-fly ones. Take a fine set of long-nosed pliers and carefully press the barb to the hook-shank. On some types of hooks, the barb will mash down against the shank; on others, most of the barb will snap off. In either event, you will now hook more trout because the finer point will penetrate more easily, and I find that the hooked-and-lost percentage doesn't rise perceptibly. Since you now won't have to wrestle with your dry fly to remove it from the fish, its hackles won't get slimy or mashed and you won't have to waste so much time changing flies during a hatch. Most important of all, though, your released fish—especially the small ones—will have a far better chance of survival.

Carry your yellow-lensed shooting glasses with you on summer evenings and use them instead of your polaroids at dusk. They'll allow you to see your dry fly fifteen to twenty minutes longer—which may help you take the best fish of the day.

Don't put your dry fly in the little keeper-ring just ahead of the cork handle. This tends to mash the hackles down to the hook-shank and hastens the death of the fly. The first, or stripping, guide is usually of the bridge type which stands out well from the rod and is a much better place for your fly while you're traveling from pool to pool. If you want to keep your leader-line connection out of the tip guide, hook your fly in first, run your leader back around the reel and then wind up the slack line.

When buying your next fly reel, choose one that is open pillared or does not have a circular line-guide. This device may do a fair job of distributing the line evenly across the spool, but you can do better by hand. When reeling with your right hand, hold your rod with the thumb and first three fingers of your left, and run the incoming line through the first bend in your lowered little finger while moving it slowly from side to side. This manual level-winding technique becomes a reflex action in a short time and is a great help when you're using a fly rod for salmon, bonefish or any large species that will take you deep into your backing.

Make the curve casts, both positive and negative, your standard presentations when dry-fly fishing. They are the most effective ones in ninety-nine out of one hundred situations and you will deliver them more accurately if you execute them automatically, without thinking.

Unless you're trying for extremely long distance, stop your rod's forward progress at forty-five degrees when dry-fly casting. This will cut down drag in two ways. It will help your fly hit the water before your line does and it will keep several more feet of line-belly off the water and out of the nearby currents.

The Turle knot, or any good knot that grasps the shank of the hook, is best for all types of fly-fishing. It will keep the fly in line with the leader, the way the old snelled flies used to do, while the popular clinch knot will not.

If you do a lot of trout-fishing, don't wade wet: the cold water can raise merry hell with the veins and circulation in your legs. Theodore Gordon's legs were in terrible shape before he reached fifty because he usually fished in summer without boots or waders.

When you're fishing in the morning, stay as far away as possible from other fishermen. In the evening, a frightened fish will probably soon come out and feed again, but a trout that has been chased into his hiding place at eleven or twelve will probably spend the rest of the day there.

Always reel in slack line with the rod-butt against your belly. This will keep the rod from wobbling violently and perhaps throwing a loop of loose line around itself. If this should happen when you're winding up after dark, it could easily smash the tip.

When you put on a new dry fly, cast it a short distance up-current and watch it carefully as it floats down past you. This may take a few seconds, but it's far better than fishing the fly for an hour before discovering that it always lands on its head or that its tail sinks every time it hits the water.

Use stiff leader material; it will give you better control of your presentation. Limp nylon may be better for the occasional lazy S cast, but it also picks up wind knots too easily.

Don't strike too quickly when fishing the dry fly. When small fish splash at your fly during the afternoon, the tendency is to strike quicker, and therefore harder, as the frustration increases. The first good fish to take securely is then sure to be broken off on the strike. The few times I have let good trout take a dry fly without interference, they have pulled out three to five feet of slack line before ejecting the fly and half of them even hooked themselves.

If you do take home a few trout, treat them well and cook them properly. Frying, or *sauté muniere;* is the best for all trout under fourteen inches. Do not put them in the pan freshly caught: they will curl up, split open and cook poorly. Wait several hours until rigor mortis has set in or even come and gone. Don't try to fry them in butter, either. It won't hold a high enough heat before it starts to turn black, and the only thing worse than an undercooked trout is a burned one. White bacon fat is best, and be generous with it. When this is hot—just below the smoking point—moisten the trout, roll them in flour and put them in. Tilt the pan from time to time to get the hot fat into the body cavities. Turn occasionally, but cook on each side for eleven or twelve minutes—a total of twenty-two to twenty-four minutes. When done, flip them out onto a paper towel to drain for a few moments. Now they should be nearly as stiff as a stick and they will be the best you have ever tasted.

17

THE LAST WORD

Most of this book has been devoted to an unorthodox method of dry-fly fishing and an explanation of how, when and why it works. I have dealt with the basic, and usually most effective, method of manipulating the floating fly, but I am certain that inventive anglers will find many variations on this theme and that the last word on the fluttering fly won't be spoken or written for a long time. I am also certain that fishermen who have read this far will have several questions they'd like to ask so I'll try to anticipate and answer some of these in this last chapter.

Is this method too difficult for the average fly-fisher? I don't think it's any more demanding than fishing the dry fly properly and drag-free in an upstream direction. That, as you may remember, takes a long time to master—or even partly master. Even a mediocre fly caster has already acquired enough control over rod and line to fish the twitched fly effectively after a very few minutes of serious practice.

The only fly-fishing method I can think of that is any easier than the twitch is the across and downstream presentation of a wet fly in a smooth, medium current. The upstream, dead-drift nymph technique—a rival method of prospecting for nonrising trout in low water—is by far the most difficult of all. Compared to this, the twitch is as easy as falling off a slippery rock.

How much of the time should you fish the twitched dry fly? This, of course, depends on where and when you do your fishing. If you go out only at dusk in summertime when the spinners are falling to the water, you may never use it at all. If you fish on rich water that teems with small mayflies and regularly rising trout, you may have to try it only occasionally on especially stubborn fish. If, however, you fish on water where caddis are important or even predominant and if you go out at times of day when few fish or no fish are showing at the surface, you might be wise to make the twitch your standard presentation.

Is this technique a new and original invention? The answer is that, of course, it can't possibly be—although I'll admit that for a while I thought I'd discovered the wheel. Many thousands of frustrated fly-fishers must have given their flies a little nudge as it floated down toward a good trout after twenty or thirty untouched offerings. But as far as I know, no one has pursued this method, systematized it or studied how and why it works, and then written it up for the benefit of other anglers.

I had known for years that trout didn't always do what they were supposed to do, but it took me a long time to put the puzzling pieces together into a meaningful picture. In earlier chapters, I described the events that led to my present theory, but certainly this was the hard way to work out a system for fishing the floating fly with an enticing element of motion. Almost every worthwhile book on trout fishing published in this century gives some hints about the killing qualities of the moving dry fly.

George M. L. LaBranche made a start in this direction and probably would have come up with a behavioristic dry-fly theory of his own if he hadn't switched his attention to salmon and bonefish shortly after completing *The Dry Fly and Fast Water*. His "bounce cast," a side-arm delivery that skipped the fly along the surface before it finally came to rest, produced much the same effect on the trout as the twitch does. LaBranche said it was absolutely murderous when he could make the delivery correctly. But even that master caster couldn't pull the stunt off very often and he finally abandoned its use. As far as I know, he never experimented with other ways of creating this same effect with the fly on the water.

Hewitt's Neversink Skaters were another experiment in this area, but I think he missed the wider possibilities of a moving dry fly because he thought these highly effective floaters were imitations of butterflies. As you may remember, Skaters are tied with two large hackles on a very small, light hook and are manipulated quite rapidly, in a stop-and-go manner, across a pool. These flies don't look like much when at rest so the tantalizing motion has to be vigorous to be effective. The method can be killing under certain conditions—especially on stocked trout—but I think this system works because it simulates the behavior of giant stone flies and crane flies rather than the antics of the much-less-common butterfly.

Roderick Haig-Brown writes that the twitch he sometimes produces, inadvertently, while mending his line in extremely fast water, often raises good fish that had let the fly pass by on previous casts. He adds that if this motion is violent or pronounced, the rise is usually a false one. This has been my experience, too. Overmanipulating your fly can be self-defeating.

Schwiebert makes a brief reference to a German friend who skittered a caddis across the water at dusk with telling effect, but the appearance of the fly and the method of skittering go unexplained. Most trout-fishing books make some mention of trout rising to a moving dry fly, but the method is never explored. It almost seems as if everyone were afraid to challenge the dead-drift dictum of the great Halford.

Is twitch-fishing sporting? In terms of consideration for your fellow anglers, it most certainly is. This across-stream technique works best from the edge of the water, and your passing along the stream in this manner will put down fewer fish and give a following fisherman a far better chance.

But is it a sporting way to take trout? I don't know how to answer this question without asking a few right back. Is it considered unsporting to give some motion to a bass bug? Is it bad form to manipulate a wet fly or streamer? I have never heard any fisherman answer these questions in the affirmative. Action imparted by the skill of the angler should, if anything, increase the quality of the sport.

I have, I'll admit, drawn a bit of flak from some sections of the establishment for fishing this way, though. A few years ago I was a guest at a posh trout club when I ran into a large, beefy gentleman standing in the middle of a pool. As I started to by-pass him through the bushes, he called over to me.

"There's a very good trout under that willow," he said. "He's come up several times in the last half hour. I've chucked everything in the box at him, but he's not having any. Why don't you try him?"

Was this man one of those rare near-saints, I wondered? Or was he just an ordinary mortal who desperately needed the satisfaction of seeing someone else fail on the fish he'd slaved over? I declined his offer politely, but when he became unpleasantly insistent, I placed him clearly in the second category and not very near the top of that.

It was to be a command performance. I waded out thirty feet upstream of him, silently reciting the names of great, but departed, anglers as a sort of riverside rosary. Then I pitched my small caddis two feet above the drooping branch he'd pointed out, twitched the fly briskly and held my breath. The trout came up as if it were on tracks!

I almost hated myself for the casualness I affected as I released that sixteen-incher. My companion's face turned bright red and he began muttering about an unprintable son of a salmon that had fallen for a dragging fly, and hinted at heresy or worse.

Perhaps there is much in what he said, but I look at it this way: if this be heresy, make the most of it. And I have been doing just that for years.

INDEX

INDEX